overwhelmed

The Self-Care Guide For College Students

Dr. Raushannah Johnson-Verwayne

Printed in the United States of America
2020 First Edition
10 9 8 7 6 5 4 3 2 1

Subject Index:
Dr. Johnson-Verwayne, Raushannah
Title: Overwhelmed: The Self-Care Guide for College
       Students
1. African American College Students 2. College &
University Student Life 3. Mental Health 4. College
Guide 5. Self-help 6. Teen & Young Adult College Guide
7. Motivation 8. Community College 9. Online Learning

Paperback ISBN: 978-0-578-76589-1
Library of Congress Card Catalog Number: 2020914480

askdrrj.com
selfcareforthecollegestudent.com

Praises For Overwhelmed...

"Self-care is everywhere! But this book really hits the mark when it comes to supporting the needs of the collegiate student. As an educator and mother of a college student, this is a must-have reference for all. Dr. Verwayne has delivered once again."

Yolanda Blackshear, Educator

"*Overwhelmed* is a powerful and comprehensive resource that empowers students of color for success in college and beyond. Dr. RJ beautifully blends real-life solutions with evidence-based research to provide beacons of light in collegiate tunnels of darkness. Darkness, unfortunately, that is especially prevalent in communities of color who, for decades, have struggled with dealing with "taboo" issues. Dr. RJ shatters these generational curses with practical, constructive, and healthy solutions for young student leaders to not only heal, but hope."

Rasheed Ali Cromwell,
JD – President, The Harbor Institute

This book is amazing and is exactly what college students need to balance their lives and mental well-being. I love how Dr. RJ has tapped into the major areas of concern that impact students as they matriculate through college. This guide is outstanding and makes self-care fun, easy, and manageable. I plan to use it in my work with students. Every clinician working with college students should read and recommend this book.

Vivian Barnette, Ph.D., ABPP

Dr. Raushannah Johnson-Verwayne

To all of the evolving young adults who are emulating

Linda Carol Brown's legacy. Your courage, boldness, innovation,

and entrepreneurial spirit is an inspiration. Press on.

Acknowledgments

On the eve of the release of *Stress, Lies, and Vacancy: The Self-Care Guide to Re-fill Your Empty Vessel*, I had the pleasure of moderating a panel called, "Loving The Skin You're in" at my alma mater. Upon interacting so intimately with bright college students from all over the United States, I realized that these secure and re- salient spirits were more fragile than any- one would ever know. The juxtaposition of confidence and anxiety, bravery and depression, self-control, and self-destruction was eye-opening. Students made it clear that they desired and needed guidance and direction for self-care, balance, and joy. Of- ten, parents assume that young adults have no worries and have no reason to worry or stress about anything. The unintended out- come is a cycle of invalidation, secrecy, and isolation resulting in a perpetual state of "overwhelmed."

To my alma mater, the illustrious North Carolina Agricultural and Technical State University, thank you for building my confidence, shaping me, and making me proud to be a part of a long-lasting legacy of Black excellence. To the Department of Psychology, thank you for making me into one of the best clinical psychologists all around.

To the Alpha Phi Chapter of Alpha Kappa Alpha Sorority, Incorporated, you groomed me and pushed me and demanded nothing less than excellence every single time. My undergraduate experience was life-changing. The lessons I learned are with me today, and those of you who came before me and along with me inhabit an irreplaceable space in my heart. You are forever held "in the highest esteem."

To my college BFF Carla, life presents us with the necessary lessons and perfect timing. I wish the gift of a friendship like ours to every college student who reads this book.

To Kamryn, Craig Jr., Jordyn, Kaylan, Rachel, and John ("Trey"), I am grateful to have had your insight, transparency, and expertise to ignite me during this process. Although I can remember my college days like they were just yesterday, things are indeed different, and your input was priceless.

To all of the college students I've encountered through The Harbor Institute programs, each of you have added to me in ways you could never imagine. Your energy and openness influenced this project from start to finish.

To my children Adriana and Ryan, watching you grow and become more aware of this world motivates me to actively contribute to the health and wellness of as many people as possible. You are both amazing in so many ways, and I am blessed and honored to be your mother. I'm looking forward to your journey.

To my husband, Adrian, thank you for sharing me with the world. I know it isn't easy. You make me better.

Table of Contents

Foreword

D r. Raushannah Johnson-Verwayne's latest book, *Overwhelmed: The Self-Care Guide for College Students*, provides a timely extensive coverage of relevant topics ranging from advice on taking a gap year and strategies for dealing with freshman week, to the ultimate goal of college graduation.

Some of the topics include time management, strategies, and techniques for stress management and anxiety, decision making, risky behaviors, and racial and gender identity. The book emphasizes the sudden freedom of college students, which necessitates proper time management. Good time management can minimize unavoidable stress. In the chapter on stress, Dr. RJ states: "You've probably been functioning at chronic stress levels so long that you don't even realize it – it's your normal." She provides tested and effective methods to manage your stress and anxiety. She talks about rational decision making and risky behaviors of college students, and anchors those real and honest conversations on developmental stages, opportunities to learn from "mistakes," and taking responsibility for the potential long-term consequences of your behaviors. The chapter on identity is critical for self-care. After all, if you do not know yourself, you cannot take care of yourself. Dr. RJ does an excellent job of explaining identity development. This chapter sets her book apart from the other self-care books.

Overwhelmed reads like a one-on-one conversation with a highly trained professional, yet it is not littered with unnecessary academic jargon. There are some self-assessments, and the "Talk Space" testimonials will speak to you about not being alone in your journey. It speaks to college students, but there are also conversations with college counselors, college administrators, and, most importantly, the conversations end with the parents.

Dr. Raushannah Johnson-Verwayne

It is refreshing and rewarding to see one of my prized students, now teaching the professor. I highly recommend this book to everyone.

George S. Robinson, Jr., Ph.D., Chairman
Department of Psychology
North Carolina A&T State University

It's A Different World...

Dear College Student,

It's Monday morning. Freshman orientation is over. Mom and dad are gone. Real-life be- gins. You ask yourself, "What will my collegiate years be like?" "Can I do it?" "Will I let everyone down?" "Will I let myself down?"

Times are different. Being a college student comes in many different forms, not just the tra- dition of being dropped off on campus for the next four years. You may live at home and at- tend a two-year college or decide to complete your degree online. You may even be considered a non-traditional student who decided to enter the workforce before completing a degree.

If you're a first-generation college student, then you may feel completely alone with lingering re- sponsibility to those back home and an unwav- ering pressure to succeed. If your parents went to college, they have no idea about the intensity of *your college experience. Their glamorized memories are akin to scenes from **School Daze** and **A Different World**, along with a highly anticipated annual Homecoming where they relive the good times from the '90s.*

But for you, the pressure is on. You're competing globally, and the stakes are high. Competition is fierce. Everyone is at the top of their class in their respective cities. Young entrepreneurs are pitching their business ideas around campus and are only two clicks away from being Instagram famous.

For ladies, your 8 AM lab preparation consists of perfect lash extensions, contoured faces, flawless hair, a to-die-for outfit, and model-ready bodies. For guys, you might be worried if your sneakers will get a crease on the long-walk to campus. You say to yourself, "what's the big deal?" but deep down on the inside, you wonder if your laid-back worldview will be enough in this new world.

Although you did well in high school, this is a new level of coursework and responsibility.

overwhelmed

Professors aren't easily impressed. Parents want to see a return on their investment. And if that isn't enough, you also have to become an adult overnight. You're just beginning to realize how much your mom did for you in high school. All of a sudden, you have to feed yourself, do laundry, stay healthy, keep your dorm clean, navigate the roommate situation, make good grades, socialize, avoid risky situations, find life-long friends, live the college dream, look good while doing it, post it on Instagram — then delete it.

With all of these distractions, your mental health is probably at the bottom of your to-do list and nowhere to be found on your vision board. Before long, stress takes its toll, anxiety and depression set in, and all of a sudden, you're OVERWHELMED.

You are not alone. Each year millions of students feel this way. That is why I have created this self-care guide just for you. You can use it as a roadmap to help you navigate these next four (or five or six) years and beyond. Self-care never goes out of style. I'm here to help diminish tha overwhelmed feeling and provide guidance and support for you to enjoy your college experience while gaining the knowledge and skills to become happy, healthy, thriving adults.

Sincerely,

Dr. RJ

About this book

Use this book as a guide to help you deal with the everyday challenges of college life. Keep going back to a topic that you struggle with, like Time Management or Mental Health. As you will soon find out, there are so many distractions throughout your college experience to pull you away from the ultimate goal — graduation.

Whether you are attending a two or four-year college, community college, or taking classes online, the pressure to minimize distractions and finish is at an all-time high. Making new friends, pledging, alco- hol, drugs, sex, work-study, and oh yeah, your college course load, are just some of balancing and juggling acts that you have to manage the moment your parents drive off. Good decision-making and creating a productive routine is a great first step towards being a responsible adult.

Doing your best to achieve as many tasks and goals each week, while enjoying the sights and sounds of the college experience is a precursor to less overall stress.

I engaged a focus group of several college students at each leg of the journey: freshman through senior year. None of the students had a self-care regimen, and all agreed that their college or university could do a better job in handling mental health issues. Summaries of our conversations appear in appropriate sections titled "Talk Space. I spoke to several moms of college students, and questions and responses to those conversations are toward the end, under the header, "My Mom Said." Finally, there is a message for college counselors to step up to the plate and help provide more effec- tive mental health solutions for students. Ongoing dialogue and initiatives to provide services and support to you must be high on the administration's agenda.

Your school wants you to graduate. Your parents and professors want you to succeed.

Yet you must want to do well and finish more than anyone else. I want you to know that you are not alone on this journey. Everyone feels overwhelmed during the highschool to college transition. Your process can and will be manageable if you create and execute your plan early. You are the dream fulfilled. Stay positive. Stay focused. You got this!

Oh, about this Gap Year thing...

I n recent years, many students and parents have talked about a gap year. After all, Malia Obama did it, so shouldn't we at least consider it? Well, from a psychologist's perspective, I'll just say that it's complicated.

Some studies have shown that people who take a gap year, particularly after a high-stress advanced placement high school year, earn higher grades than their counterparts who entered college directly after high school. However, those who can afford to take a year off to travel abroad generally have several other "protective factors" that contribute to favorable results. Other pros include the following: 1) the chance to gain new skills, 2) the ability to earn money, 3) meeting new people and making new connections, 4) self-discovery and clarity,

5) independence and 6) increased foreign language skills.

A true gap year is designed to be a semester or year of experiential learning to deepen personal, practical, or professional awareness. A gap year is not intended to just chill. Some cons of a gap year include the following: 1) A "real" gap year can be quite expensive, 2) the risk of losing momentum and motivation, 3) the pressure of feeling "behind" peers, 4) many universities do not accept a gap year of deferment, 5) possible social disconnect from friends, or 6) difficulty adjusting to the rigor of college life upon return.

My advice...a gap year is a highly individualized choice. Discuss the pros and cons with your parents and school advisors and determine if a gap year is appropriate for you. Remember that a gap year is not a "break." There's nothing wrong with taking a break to work, save money, take classes at a community college, gain experience, or meet other obligations. However, a break is just that, time off. A gap year is time *on*. Choose accordingly.

Pop Quiz...

What is Self-Care?
A) Caring about yourself
B) Eating healthy, exercising, and proper sleep
C) Time Management
D) All of the above

Answer on page 196

Question: Is the topic of self-care relevant for college students?

"Yeah, I think it is. I was so caught up in my schoolwork and doing hair on the side that I never took time out for myself. I am loyal, and I was there for my friends no matter what. I realized that I was going 90 miles an hour for everyone and everything except me!"

"Yes, it's something we need to talk about. You have to make goals for the week and try to stick to them. In my senior year, it's like the four years just went by, and I never took time to sit, reflect, and pause. I pressured myself too hard to fit in and get things done, but I struggled with making time for myself in-between."

"I think it would have been more effective if it were taught in high school so that you can carry it on to college. We all need to reflect and focus on our goals often."

"I noticed that my school is talking more about mental health and advising us to take out time each day to meditate or pray when you start your day or when you end the day."

"I also agree with the high school comment be-because we are stressing more to get into college. It's very competitive and harder to get into college. I think people are smarter, more athletic, and their SAT and ACT scores are high. So self-care should have definitely been talked about more in my high school because junior and senior year were very stressful."

I: Time Management

CHAPTER 1

Syllabus Shock 101

If you're like I was the first year, the moment you receive the syllabus, your heart begins to race. Your palms become sweaty as you flip each page or continuously scroll down on your laptop. Then your mind immediately switches to what's next from your other courses. *Is this a joke? How can this professor expect me to complete all of this work for **one** class?* After the shock wears off, you scan the room to see if anyone else is experiencing panic mode like you. Trying to read the faces and body language of complete strangers is challenging. *Am I the only one who thinks this is too much? There's no way the professor can grade all this!* In the back of your mind, you hear your high school guidance counselor's voice, "Listen up, when you get to college, you're going t have a lot of work to do in a short amount of time. It's about buckling down and focusing. You can do it if you really want to graduate!"

Welcome to "Syllabus Shock 101." Whether you are the student who got straight A's, B's or C's, or the student who barely got by, the reality of balancing college courses while navigating the social, emotional, and financial prerequisites to survive the next four years are daunting. Not to mention managing life's incidents beyond your control, such as family issues back home or a global pandemic that has shifted our "normal" way of life. It's no surprise that many students lack time management skills. Most of us did not learn how to manage our time before we arrived on campus. Don't be discouraged. Time management is a challenge for adults, but it will set the stage for your future at this moment in your life.

As a college student, failure to adopt a structured plan to complete your major could lead to dropping courses because you are just too far behind. This only prolongs your ultimate goal — graduation date. The sooner you embrace a time management regimen, the more likely you will be able to not only survive college but thrive. As you will see, the goal is to thrive. Surviving takes a lot more work, stress, and less discipline. A large part of self-care is balancing tasks and responsibilities. Say to yourself; *I have to find the right balance. Today is the perfect time to balance my college dreams into reality.*

CHAPTER 2

Who's Checking For You?

Y ou have the same 24 hours in a day as your classmates to cross items off your "to-do lists," spend time with friends and family, and have personal downtime. One thing for sure, planning ahead and us- ing your time wisely can help you get more done without added stress. Every student needs a reasonable time management plan to get to the end of the semester with your sanity intact.

Grab a notebook and pen or just use your phone. Now may be a good moment to in- vest in a time management app. There are several free apps available. The best way to know which one works for you is to read re- views, ask around, and then download the one that connects with you. Try it out for at least two weeks. If some functions or features are not helpful, then switch to another one. Don't procrastinate on finding an app or using a traditional method of paper and pen to create a schedule. Remember, balancing responsibilities is not easy, and no one is an expert—not even your parents. The most important thing is to at least try to create a plan and set goals to ease the stress overload *before* midterms.

One of the hardest challenges of the college experience is meeting assignment deadlines and being prepared for exams. Most students find the time to party, hang out, eat and sleep, yet wait until the absolute last minute to get work done. College creates more distractions than you'll ever imagine. When you were in high school, regardless of the extracurricular activities, weekend parties, and even your part-time job, you still went home to your parents' house and followed the house's rules. You might even admit that the once annoying imposed structure and routine are greatly missed and may have been taken for granted.

Now you're in free-fall. There is an activity happening on campus and off-campus seven days a week, all day and night. And guess what? No one is checking on you! This unknown freedom to show up when you want to, show out if you want to, or sleep the day away, has consequences. What's taking up most of your time? Start thinking about the things you do each day that are time-wasters, things that keep you from being productive. For students, I believe the number one time-waster is your smartphone.

- How often are you checking social media? Who are you checking for? Who's checking for you?

- Are you texting and taking calls when you should be studying?

- Do you surf the web when you should be outlining a chapter?

If any of these smartphone time-wasters jump out to you, then you have to write them down. It's goal-setting time. Don't torture yourself and write that you will *never* check social media while studying. Since this is a new discipline, it will take time to limit social media checks while studying to become a habit. Start by putting your phone on silent and tucking it away in a desk drawer or your backpack for at least an hour. You'll be surprised by how much work you can get done with focusing for one hour with no distractions. When the urge hits you to check your phone, set a timer for 15 minutes. Try to stick to this type of routine for at least a week. Your progress in your studies should be the encouragement you need to continue. Keep in mind that this is just a few hours of your day. As you are working on your full schedule, consider two hours a day to studying during the week and four or five hours on the weekends. You will have plenty of time to socialize and party.

CHAPTER 3

Plan Ahead Or Plan To Fail

Take a serious look at your coursework. Create a "reminder" of all deadlines on your phone at least one week *before* the due date. Plan your day in a way that allows you to be flexible yet structured enough to accomplish at least two goals for the day, such as limiting social media and arriving to class on time.

Once you have solidified your course schedule, then write out your plan for the month. Your plan should include your actual class meeting times, breaks to eat, as well as 15-minute breaks (if possible) between classes to review your notes for the upcoming class to refresh your memory.

When it comes to large assignments, prioritize completing milestones to turn in the assignment on time. Do your best to complete longer assignments early so that you can review them over the next few weekends. Review your schedule at least twice a day to help you stay on track. During the evenings, review the next day's schedule to stimulate your mind about what lies ahead.

Start Small

It can work to your advantage to finish smaller projects first and tackle large projects or big exams. Starting small will increase your confidence and give you the momentum needed to handle the large assignments. The longer you wait to do small assignments, the more likely stress and feelings of being overwhelmed creep in. You will probably not do as well if you rush or wait until the last minute to do the small tasks, which are bonus points from the professor. Don't sweat the small stuff...just get it done!

Multitasking

Juggling multiple assignments increases your chances of being less productive. A study by the University of London demonstrated that our IQ drops similar to someone who did not get a good night's sleep when we multitask. [1] Focus until you finish. Don't start a new task until you complete a good portion of your coursework goal for the day.

There's an old saying which still guides me today; "A jack of all trades is a master of nothing." Be a master...of something.

Sleep Deprivation

College students generally expect sleep deprivation to be a part of the college experience. Up to 60% of all college students suffer from poor sleep quality, and 7.7% meet all criteria of an insomnia disorder. While there may be periods where studying will be intense, sleep deprivation is not only unnecessary; it is potentially dangerous. According to the National Sleep Foundation, being awake for 18 hours produces an impairment equal to a blood alcohol concentration (BAC) of .05, and .10 after 24 hours; .08 is considered legally drunk.[2] So, if you are worried about drinking and driving, it is only logical to add sleepy and driving to the list of "never dos."

Sleep deprivation is simply defined as not getting enough sleep to feel rested. Teens need about 9 to 10 hours of sleep, and adults need approximately 7 to 8 hours of sleep; however, sleep needs can significantly vary from person to person. It should also be noted that adolescent brains can have a later natural sleep-wake cycle. Sleep deprivation is not the same as being a "night owl."

It can result in impaired judgment, mood changes, motor vehicle accidents, memory and concentration issues, lower grade point averages, and academic failure. Erratic sleep/wake cycles can also trigger episodes of depression or anxiety. Sleep is not a luxury; it is a necessity. Don't feel pressured to "pull all-nighters." Adequate preparation and time management can reduce the need to study by cramming.

Question: Is college what you expected it to be?

The majority of the students felt it was what they expected. A few thought the work would be harder and was surprised that the work was generalized.

"I thought everything was based upon my major. I hated freshman year. I had no room for error. I did not factor in what it is like as an adult for the first time. Not having my parents doing everything for me. I did not expect it to be such a challenge, but it was!"

"It was a challenge for me because I had to bal-

ance being a student and cheering."

"College was so hyped up. Freshman Week was everything! Then after the first month, it hit me,

oh, this is how it's supposed to be. I need to get to work now. I was already used to being away from home, so that part was OK."

"Once Freshman Week died down, I was worried about maintaining my scholarship, so I hit the books. Yes, I was excited to be away from home, but I really missed my family. I am very close to my family."

"OMG, my parents went to my college. My sister attended as well, and then it was my turn. Everyone hyped it up. My sister loved every second of it. I was a little disappointed, but for me, it was really about graduating."

Question: What is one thing you wish you would have been told about college?

Most of the students reiterated how their parents warned them about sex and drugs, but no one advised them about self-care or taking a moment out to breathe, relax and enjoy the experience because you can never get those years back.

RAUSHANNAH JOHNSON-VERWAYNE

"Freshman week does not last forever! I was in Freshman Week for the first month, and I realized that I needed to kick it in gear and make time for grind and work mode. I was hanging with people who were there to have fun and party. I had to change my circle quickly!"

"I wish I would have been told to have more fun because time flies. The four years is a short amount of time you will never get that again."

"I wish someone told freshman year to step out of my comfort zone. I only went to one main event. I realize now that I could have made more friends and run for more positions. I shrink behind others, and now I am in my senior year, and I wish I would have done more."

"Figure out areas in your schedule for just you. Take time for yourself to relax. I thought I was prepared for the workload. I messed up with my

time. I was attending parties every weekend. I needed to take time for myself and just breathe to get ready for each week."

Pop Quiz

Stress Test

Answers provided on page 196

Dr. Raushannah Johnson-Verwayne

How Stressed Are You?

Note: This scale is not a clinical diagnostic instrument and is provided for self-awareness only. It merely identifies some of the symptoms of stress that you may be unaware of. If you have any concerns about the results, please contact your primary care physician or therapist.

0) Never 1) Sometimes 2) Often 3) Always

1. I feel tired:_____
2. I use caffeine or nicotine: _____
3. I have sleep problems (i.e. falling asleep, staying asleep, or restless sleep):_____
4. I get headaches: _____
5. I have stomach issues (i.e. nausea, vomiting, diarrhea, constipation, gas, irritable bowel) : _____
6. I find it hard to make decisions : _____
7. I forget little things (i.e. where I put my keys, details, names) : _____
8. I find it hard to concentrate : _____
9. I am irritable and easily annoyed : _____
10. I have back or neck pain/stiffness/discomfort : _____
11. I have mood swings or feel overly emotional : _____
12. I eat too much or too little : _____
13. I feel overwhelmed and helpless : _____
14. I find it hard to relax or wind down : _____
15. My work performance has declined and/or I have trouble completing things : _____

Score:

0-11 Keep up the good work. It looks like you don't sweat the small stuff

12-23 Be careful. Little things are starting to add up.

24-35 Warning; a score in this range suggests you may be experiencing a moderate to high level of stress.

36-45 It's time to make some immediate changes. This score suggests that you're in the danger zone.

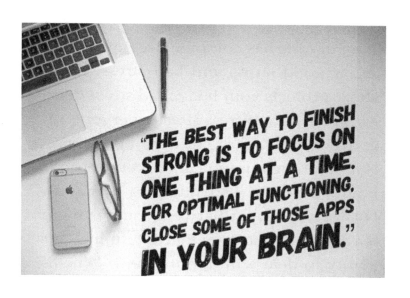

"THE BEST WAY TO FINISH STRONG IS TO FOCUS ON ONE THING AT A TIME. FOR OPTIMAL FUNCTIONING, CLOSE SOME OF THOSE APPS IN YOUR BRAIN."

CHAPTER 4

Stress Battle

Everyone has common stressors. There is good stress and bad stress. Good stress protects your body. Bad stress damages your body. Stress affects everyone, regardless of age, race, culture, or religion. It is a natural communication between our brain and body responding to demands. For every situation that we encounter, there is a demand or stressor that determines our ability to deal with the incident. Whether it's our family, school, life changes, or trauma, all of these everyday events can be stressful.

Stress also magnifies negative thoughts. So if you receive a lower grade than you expected, you may see it as a complete failure rather than an opportunity for improvement. Every time there is a perceived tressor, your brain instantly goes into an active cycle of transmitting information to your body. Once the stressor goes away, you return to a calm state. For some of us, stress triggers happen occasionally. For others, maybe a few times each week. Yet, for many of you, stress triggers are operating in chronic stress mode, so you never get to experience that calm state.

You've probably been functioning at chronic stress levels for so long that you don't even realize it — it's your normal. When this happens, your body is undergoing physiological changes that make you more susceptible to physical ailments like diabetes, high blood pressure, obesity, insomnia, irritable bowel syndrome, anxiety, and depression — all because you are *unknowing- ly* triggering a constant panic attack. Your body is telling you to run, fight, or hide.

The good news is that despite all of the negative impacts of stress, you have the power to fix it! Your brain has neuroplasticity, which means that it can be retrained and reprogrammed. Chronic stress can change the brain structurally and functionally, yet therapy and treatment can also change the brain in the same manner. Therefore, the negative impacts of stress on our physical and emotional health can be reversed over time and lead to a healthier lifestyle.

To Manage Your Stress

- **Listen to your body: Pay close attention to how your body responds to stressors.** Are you sleeping at night? Are you easily angered? Are you binge eating at night? Are you engaging in destructive behaviors like drug and alcohol use that is out of your norm?

- **Engage in more physical fitness activity:** Exercise and weights, walking, swimming, and biking, or even Zumba.

- **Choose mindful, relaxing activities:** Meditation, yoga, Tai Chi, painting, drawing, and hobbies. Create a vision board and celebrate the little things.

- **Prioritize:** Set realistic goals for the day or the week.

- **Seek Fellowship:** Connect with people who can provide emotional and other support, such as helping out with various responsibilities or healthy distractions.

- **Contact your school health center to speak with a licensed therapist**.

II: Mental Health Check-In

Pop Quiz

Toxic or Typical?

1. Staying awake all night on a regular basis
2. Making sure every hour of your day is filled with something to do
3. Using THC daily to help with agitation or to help you calm down
4. Nonstop worry or stress
5. Feeling overwhelmed most of the time
6. Problems concentrating
7. Missing class at least once a week
8. Using substances to help you escape uncomfortable feelings
9. Daily headaches and/or stomachaches
10. Constant fear of failure

Answers provided on page 196

CHAPTER 5

Attention-Deficit/ Hyperactivity Disorder (ADHD)

A DHD is a common mental disorder diagnosed in children (more common in boys) but affects many adults. Symptoms include inattention (not being able to keep focus), hyperactivity (excess movement that is not fitting to the setting), and impulsivity (hasty acts that occur at the moment without thought).[3] ADHD is more than being disorganized, forgetful, and "messy." When untreated, ADHD can trigger other disorders such as anxiety, depression, or substance abuse.

ADHD is diagnosed as one of three types: inattentive type, hyperactive/impulsive type, or combined type.[4] This diagnosis comes from obtaining information from parents, teachers, and primary care physicians. Adults with ADHD are treated with medication, psychotherapy, or a combination. There are also behavior management strategies, which focus on minimizing distractions and increasing structure. In addition, nutrition plays a significant role in managing ADHD, mainly Omega 3, 6, and 9 fatty acids. If you have been diagnosed with ADHD as a child, continue to seek treatment as an adult.

- *Inattentive Type ADHD-* is often more difficult to diagnose. Generally, children and adolescents who have inattentive symptoms, especially girls, are easily overlooked and regarded as children who consistently work below their potential. Inattentive Type ADHD is the former "ADD" and can look like the following: being a perfectionist, being silly or talkative, daydreaming, feeling anxious or sad, having trouble maintaining friendships, or acting shy. Often Inattentive Type ADHD is misdiagnosed as a learning disability.

- *Combined Type ADHD* - combines both Inattentive and Hyperactive/Impulsive Type. This type of ADHD often involves risk-taking, poor decision-making, defiance, and subsequent feelings of defeat.

Managing ADHD

* Create a college game plan early on

* Be strategic about choosing classes

* Plan ahead and minimize distractions

* Stay organized by using systems

* Keep a regular schedule and routine as much as possible

    * Exercise and maintain a balanced diet

    * Set up accommodations with the university counseling center

CHAPTER 6

Anxiety

A nxiety disorders are the most common mental disorders in the Unit-
ed States. An estimated 264 million peo- ple
worldwide have an anxiety disorder. [5]
People diagnosed with anxiety disorders
are dealing with a serious psychiatric disorder that involves extreme worry or fear.
Women are twice as likely affected by men,
which is partly because more women seek
treatment.

Common Anxiety Disorders:

- *Generalized anxiety disorder (GAD)*
  - when a person is excessively worried
  about a variety of things like money,
  health, work, or other issues. They
  constantly worry about disasters and
  things beyond their control. Without

medication and treatment, GAD individuals are not able to control their worry. This type of anxiety disorder comes on gradually with the highest risk between childhood and middle age. Biological factors, such as family background and stressful life experiences, contribute to those diagnosed with GAD.

- *Social anxiety disorder (social phobia)* - second most commonly diagnosed disorder affecting nearly 15 million Americans as the result of a specific phobia.[6] People diagnosed with social phobia have exhibited extreme anxiety or fear at being judged, evaluated, or rejected during a social or performance situation. There- fore, making presentations in class or other settings can be stressful as they are worried about their physi- cal appearance and every aspect of their delivery. In addition, individ- uals experience physical symptoms such as sweating, rapid heartbeat, and nausea. Research demonstrates that people living with this fear tend to be more prone to depression and alcohol abuse.

- *Panic disorder and panic attacks* - when a person has a sudden pan- ic attack and becomes preoccupied with fear that the attack will happen again. Panic disorder usually begins after age 21 and can cause a signifi- cant disruption in a person's life as they avoid situations for fear of hav- ing another attack. People diagnosed with panic disorder call out sick more often and over schedule doctor's vis- its to the point where people close to them may label them as hypochon- driacs.

Dr. Raushannah Johnson-Verwayne

Generalized Anxiety Disorder 7-item (GAD-7) scale

Date:_____Name:_____DOB: _____

Over the last 2 weeks, how often have you been bothered by the following prolems?	Not at all	Several days	Over half the days	Nearly every day
1. Feeling nervous, anxious, or on edge	0	1	2	3
2. Not being able to stop or control worrying	0	1	2	3
3. Worrying too much about different things	0	1	2	3
4. Trouble relaxing	0	1	2	3
5. Being so restless that it's hard to sit still	0	1	2	3
6. Becoming easily annoyed or irritable	0	1	2	3
7. Feeling afraid as if something awful might happen	0	1	2	3
Add the score for each column		+	+	+
Total Score *(add your column scores)* =				

If you checked off any problems, how difficult have these made it for you to do your work, take care of things at home, or get along with other people?

Not difficult at all _____
Somewhat difficult _____
Very difficult _____
Extremely difficult _____

Source: Spitzer RL, Kroenke K. Williams JBW, Lowe B. A brief measure for assessing generalized anxiety disorder. *Arch Inern Med.* 2006;166:1092-1097.

Techniques to Reduce Anxiety
Deep Breathing

You can monitor breathing by merely inhaling and exhaling several times: breathe in five seconds and breathe out five seconds. Each time you do this, you are sending a signal to your brain that everything is OK. This makes your heart rate slow down, which is the assurance that you are in a normal relaxed state. Controlled and intentional breathing is easy and simple to incorporate into your day to stop the stress response from happening.

Progressive Muscle Relaxation

* Find a comfortable position, either sitting or lying down. Make sure you will not be

interrupted. Focus only on your body and your breathing. When your mind wanders, bring it back to the muscle you are working on.

* Take a deep breath. Breathe in through your nose (inflate your abdomen like a balloon), hold for 2-3 seconds, then ex- hale slowly like deflating a balloon. As you breathe in, notice your stomach rising and your lungs filling with air.

* Repeat slowly and patiently. As you breathe out, imagine the tension in your body be- ing released and flowing out of your body.

Again breathe in… and breathe out.

* Notice the change in your heart rate and the feeling in your chest. Now tense each muscle group, one group at a time from head to toe then from toe to head. Squeeze, release, squeeze, release, and repeat.

* Become familiar with the relaxed feeling.

CHAPTER 7

Depression

Depression is a serious mental health condition that affects more women than men. This is because of women's biological, hormonal, and social differences that specifically concern us. Depression is not just feeling sad, going through a rough patch, or something that you can instantly "snap out of." Depression requires *immediate* medical care by a licensed professional. If left untreated, depression can be devastating for those individuals suffering from it as well as their families.

Often, symptoms of depression go unnoticed because depression has been paint- ed as a "super sad, crying all of the time, unable to get out of bed" condition. Depression comes in many forms and rang- es

from mild, or "low-level" to severe. All
types of depression can significantly interfere with your life, so pay attention to
any and **all** symptoms, no matter the severity.

Depression can come about as a result of
trauma or a life-changing event. In addition, depression is genetically linked, so it is
important to know your family history,
which can be challenging as discussions
around mental illness are uncomfortable
and stigmatized in the Black community.
Don't be silenced. Ask questions and speak
to family members and those you trust to
get answers and get help.

With early detection, diagnosis, and a
treatment plan taking into account a combination of medication, psychotherapy, and
lifestyle choices, most people with
depression get better and live happier. Individuals may have only one episode in a
lifetime, but for most people who have this
mental illness, depression recurs. If left
untreated, episodes can last from a few

months to several years. "There is an estimated 16 million American adults — almost 7% of the population claimed to have
had at least one major depressive episode
in the past year."[7]

overwhelmed

Patient Health Questionnaire - 9

PHQ-9 — Nine Symptom Checklist

Patient Name   **Date**

1. Over the last 2 weeks, how often have you been bothered by any of the following problems? Read each item carefully, and circle your response.

   a. Little interest or pleasure in doing things
      Not at all   **Several days**   **More than half the days**   **Nearly every day**

   b. Feeling down, depressed, or hopeless
      Not at all   **Several days**   **More than half the days**   **Nearly every day**

   c. Trouble falling asleep, staying asleep, or sleeping too much
      Not at all   **Several days**   **More than half the days**   **Nearly every day**

   d. Feeling tired or having little energy
      Not at all   **Several days**   **More than half the days**   **Nearly every day**

   e. Poor appetite or overeating
      Not at all   **Several days**   **More than half the days**   **Nearly every day**

   f. Feeling bad about yourself, feeling that you are a failure, or feeling that you have let yourself or your family down
      Not at all   **Several days**   **More than half the days**   **Nearly every day**

   g. Trouble concentrating on things such as reading the newspaper or watching television
      Not at all   **Several days**   **More than half the days**   **Nearly every day**

   h. Moving or speaking so slowly that other people could have noticed. Or being so fidgety or restless that you have been moving around a lot more than usual
      Not at all   **Several days**   **More than half the days**   **Nearly every day**

   i. Thinking that you would be better off dead or that you want to hurt yourself in some way
      Not at all   **Several days**   **More than half the days**   **Nearly every day**

2. If you checked off any problem on this questionnaire so far, how difficult have these problems made it for you to do your work, take care of things at home, or get along with other people?

   Not Difficult at All   **Somewhat Difficult**   **Very Difficult**   **Extremely Difficult**

PHQ-9 — Scoring Tally Sheet

Dr. Raushannah Johnson-Verwayne

Patient Name   **Date**

1. **Over the last 2 weeks, how often have you been bothered by any of the following problems? Read each item carefully, and circle your response.**

	Not at all	Several days	More than half the days	Nearly every day
	0	1	2	3
a. Little interest or pleasure in doing things				
b. Feeling down, depressed, or hopeless				
c. Trouble falling asleep, staying asleep, or sleeping too much				
d. Feeling tired or having little energy				
e. Poor appetite or overeating				
f. Feeling bad about yourself, feeling that you are a failure, or feeling that you have let yourself or your family down				
g. Trouble concentrating on things such as reading the newspaper or watching television				
h. Moving or speaking so slowly that other people could have noticed. Or being so fidgety or restless that you have been moving around a lot more than usual				
i. Thinking that you would be better off dead or that you want to hurt yourself in some way				
Totals				

2. **If you checked off any problem on this questionnaire so far, how difficult have these problems made it for you to do your work, take care of things at home, or get along with other people?**

Not Difficult At All	Somewhat Difficult	Very Difficult	Extremely Difficult
0	1	2	3

2 Tools

How to Score PHQ-9

Scoring Method For Diagnosis

Scoring Method For Planning And Monitoring Treatment

Major Depressive Syndrome is suggested if:
- Of the 9 items, 5 or more are circled as at least "More than half the days"
- Either item 1a or 1b is positive, that is, at least "More than half the days"

Minor Depressive Syndrome is suggested if:
- Of the 9 items, b, c, or d are circled as at least "More than half the days"
- Either item 1a or 1b is positive, that is, at least "More than half the days"

Question One
- To score the first question, tally each response by the number value of each response:

   Not at all = 0 Several days = 1

   More than half the days = 2 Nearly every day = 3
- Add the numbers together to total the score.
- Interpret the score by using the guide listed below:

Score	Action
≤4	The score suggests the patient may not need depression treatment.
> 5-14	Physician uses clinical judgment about treatment, based on patient's duration of symptoms and functional impairment.
≥15	Warrants treatment for depression, using antidepressant, psychotherapy and/or a combination of treatment

Question Two
In question two the patient responses can be one of four: not difficult at all, somewhat difficult, very difficult, extremely difficult. The last two responses suggest that the patient's functionality is impaired. After treatment begins, the functional status is again measured to see if the patient is improving.

Managing Depression

*Get adequate sleep on a regular basis

*Exercise...the more endorphins, the better

*Be sure to take a multivitamin, especially vitamins D and B-complex

*See your therapist regularly

*Practice daily positive affirmations

*Keep a gratitude journal

*Be aware of cognitive distortions/automatic negative thinking

Treatment for Depression

*Research suggests that mild to moderate depression responds best to psychotherapy, particularly CBT (Cognitive Behavior Therapy) and stress reduction.

*Moderate to severe depression or depression in a person who has a family history of depression responds best to CBT and medication.

*No one treatment will work alone. Our minds, bodies, and spirits all require regular attention and function better when we care for them as a whole.

Dr. Raushannah Johnson-Verwayne

Cognitive Distortions/ Limited-Thinking Patterns

1. ALL-OR-NOTHING THINKING (also known as POLARIZED THINKING): You see things in black and white categories. If your performance fails short of perfect, you see yourself as a total failure. There's no middle ground, no room for mistakes.

2. OVERGENERALIZATION: You reach a general conclusion based on a single incident or piece of evidence. You exaggerate the frequency of problems and use negative global labels.

3. FILTERING: You focus on the negative details while ignoring all the positive aspects of a situation.

4. CATASTROPHIZING: You expect, even visualize disaster. You notice or hear about a problem and think, "What if tragedy strikes?" You inappropriately exaggerate the importance of things.

5. MAGNIFYING: You exaggerate the degree or intensity of the problem. You turn up the volume on anything bad, making it loud, large, and overwhelming.

6. SHOULDS: You have a lot of ironclad rules about how you and other people should act. People who break the rules anger you, and you feel guilty when you violate the rules. You try to motivate yourself with "shoulds" and "shouldn'ts," as if you had to be punished before you could be expected to do anything. The emotional consequence is guilt.

7. PERSONALIZATION: You see yourself as the cause of some negative external event or someone's reaction for which, in fact, you were not necessarily a consideration or an important factor. You assume that everything people do or say is some kind of reaction to you. You also compare yourself to others, trying to determine who is smarter, more competent, better looking, and so on.

8. MIND READING: You arbitrarily conclude that someone is reacting negatively to you, and you don't bother to check this assumption out. Without their saying so, you know what people are feeling and why they act the way they do. In particular, you have certain knowledge of how people think and feel about you.

9. EMOTIONAL REASONING: You assume that your negative emotions necessarily reflect the way things really are: "I feel it, therefore it must be true."

10. LABELING AND MISLABELING: This is an extreme form of overgeneralization. Instead of describing your error, you attach a negative label to yourself: "I am a loser." When someone else's behavior rubs you the wrong way you attach a negative label to him or her.

11. SELECTIVE ATTENTION & SELECTIVE MEMORY: When you pay attention to information that confirms your beliefs and ignore other information that may contradict your beliefs. Selective memory is when you only remember certain pieces of information that confirm what you believe.

From Feeling Good by David Burns, M.D.; Thoughts and Feelings by McKay, Fanning, & Davis; & Shyness & Social Anxiety Workbook by Antony & Swinson

overwhelmed

CHALLENGE YOUR THINKING ERRORS:

Identify an automatic thought that causes you stress:

Label thinking error(s) if applicable:

Generate replacement thought(s):

From Feeling Good by David Burns, M.D.; Thoughts and Feelings by McKay, Fanning, & Davis; & Shyness & Social Anxiety Workbook by Antony & Swinson

Social Isolation

When a person withdraws from normal activities, this is defined as social isolation. A person can become socially isolated for several reasons, including losing friends, failing an exam, a breakup, physical or mental illness, or social anxiety. One cause for social isolation may be low self-esteem, which can lead to loneliness or other risk factors such as suicidal ideation, depression, and alcohol or drug misuse. If you or someone you know is experiencing social isolation, speak to someone you trust and make an appointment with your school's mental health center. It might even be helpful to plan ahead and create an emergency contact list at the beginning of each year and exchange lists with your roommate or a close friend.

Suicide

Every suicide is a tragedy. Although the cause of suicide is unknown, the most prominent linkage is depression. Suicide is a complex and multifaceted severe form of human behavior. Factors such as person- al and family history, neurobiology (struc- ture and function of the nervous system), stress-related events, and sociocultural ex- periences are all interrelated to this unfor- tunate outcome.

When someone is experiencing severe or long-term stress, it can become over- whelming. Functioning in a continuous cycle of stress, anxiety, trauma, or depres- sion may leave you with deep feelings of hopelessness. These negative emotions hinder your ability to see solutions to your problems, and you believe that the only remedy is to take your own life.

Careful attention must be paid to those with suicidal ideation. Whether active or pas- sive, suicidal ideation must be taken seri- ously. It's when a person's mind is in a dark place and replays thoughts of their ultimate death. Active ideation is when a person has decided they want to die and has considered the method to do so. Conversely, passive ideation can take the form of envisioning dying in your sleep, an automobile accident, or terminal illness. Either of these thoughts of death needs to be addressed immediately.

Equally important are those who attempt suicide. Often people attempt suicide as a cry for help, not so much because they really want to die. Suicide attempts tell the world, "I am in pain, I am hurting, I need to escape the pain, and I need someone to hear me and help me deal with this dev- astating emotion." Individuals who make failed attempts are at a much higher risk of trying again. Unfortunately, their sec- ond attempts more than likely prove tragic. However, with professional therapy, those who have attempted suicide can go on to live healthy, fulfilled lives. Suicide is the 4th leading cause of death for adults 18 to 65.8 Suicide rates for females are the high-est amongst those aged 45-54. Women are more likely than men to attempt suicide, yet men are more likely than women to complete suicide.

WARNING SIGNS FOR SUICIDE RISK

Emotional: "Feeling"
- feeling depressed
- lack of interest in activities once enjoyed
- irritability
- anger
- anxiety
- shame or humiliation
- mood swings

Verbal: "Talking about"
- killing themselves
- their life having no purpose
- feeling like a burden
- feeling stuck
- not wanting to exist

Behavioral: "Doing"
- isolating from others
- not communicating with friends or family
- giving away possessions or writing a will
- driving recklessly
- increased aggression
- increased drug and alcohol use
- searching about suicide on the internet
- gathering materials (pills or a weapon)

I'M EXPERIENCING THOUGHTS OF SUICIDE

- Contact the National Suicide Prevention Lifeline: **1-800-273-8255**. They also have an online chat and text. Text **"Home" to 741-741**.

- Know that you aren't alone. You aren't crazy, weak, or flawed.

- You have more pain than you can cope with right now, and although it feels overwhelming and permanent, with time and support, the pain and suicidal feelings will pass.

- Your emotions are not fixed. Pain is temporary.

- Depression has a way of tricking the brain into thinking that nothing will ever get better.

- Avoid being alone.

- Tell someone.

How to cope if you've lost a friend or loved one to suicide

1. *Accept how you're feeling:* Your emotions are valid and will vary throughout your healing process. You may feel shock, guilt, anger, shame, denial, anxiety, confusion, loneliness, and in some cases, relief.

2. *There's no timeline:* Don't worry about when you should stop feeling negative emotions or how long you are grieving. Everyone's path will be different. Focus on your needs and what you can do to heal and move forward.

3. *Self-care:* You cannot heal if you are depleted. Do your best to eat properly, get adequate sleep, exercise, yoga, meditation, or pick up a relaxing hobby.

4. *Stay connected:* Talk to and accept help from those who have been supportive to you in the past, whether

family, friends, church, or other connections.

5. *Talk to a professional:* A psychologist and other mental health professionals can help you express and manage your feelings and provide coping strategies, resources, and tools.

Question: Do you know anyone who has been a victim of suicide?

"At my university, there were 17 suicides in one year. That's pretty scary, even though it is a large school. I don't know why there has been such an increase in suicide. Maybe social media and the need to be liked by everyone, even strangers."

overwhelmed

"My friend from high school committed suicide over Thanksgiving break. That was really sad because she was a great person. Someone you would never think would feel that way, let alone do it. Our university has a mental health clinic, but students don't trust talking to the adults. Many of the counselors are older than our parents, so they have no idea what we are going through today."

"I did not really have an understanding of suicide until my close friend on campus was going through depression and talking about suicide. She was stressed all the time and missed class, saying she was not feeling well. She got a bad grade, and it made her feel worse. We went to the health center, and she was able to talk with a counselor."

"I want to believe that the university really cares about us students, but sometimes the bureaucracy shows otherwise. I had a friend who was really in a bad place. He went to the mental health center on campus, and they told him to call to make an appointment. He was devastated. When

word got out that a student was turned away, no one else wanted to go because they felt the school does not care about them. Just pay your tuition, please."

"I knew someone who committed suicide. The school sent out a letter to parents and students. There was a memorial service. Outside of that, it was business as usual. Maybe the school does not want to dwell on the bad, but it is a real issue. I think they could do a better job at prevention and offering safe spaces for students."

"There were definitely students who committed suicide in my high school. When I got to my college, they actually talk about it openly and remind us that we have access to counselors and student leadership."

"At my school, it is very easy to find yourself isolated on campus. I wish the school were more open and supportive. But if you feel isolated, you are not open to seek help. The school needs to do a better job of providing resources and preventing suicide. Professors and counselors have been insensitive to specific student problems during *this pandemic. A girl I know could not get extended time on her assignments despite proving that both of her parents have coronavirus."*

"I think there needs to be some type of forum where psychology professors and other mental health counselors of the schools have weekly or monthly events to get to know students. In order for the students to trust you and come to you for help, you have to have a relationship with them."

Dr. Raushannah Johnson-Verwayne

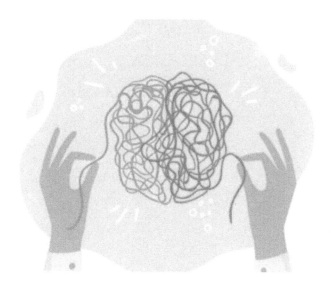

"Our bodies and brains are not designed for perfection.

If your arm is broken, see a doctor. If your

neurotransmitters are broken, see a doctor. Same thing."

— Dr. RJ

III: Decision-Making

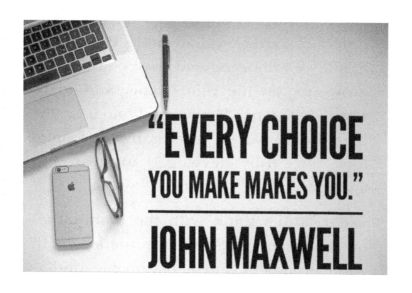

CHAPTER 8

What Was I Thinking?

D o you have that friend who scored in the top one percentile on the SAT or ACT, yet that same friend continually makes poor decisions? Is this you? The Catch-22 scenario is inevitable. On the one hand, we are urged and even chastised to grow up, do the right thing, and make good decisions. However, biologi- cally, the rational part of your brain, the frontal lobe, isn't fully developed until around age 25.

Older adults think with the brain's pre-frontal cortex to respond to situations with good judgment and a reasonable under-standing of the consequences. However, during high school to early college years, you are processing information from an emotional perspective. It's probably why most of the time, you can't explain what you are thinking because you are *feeling* versus thinking.

Your frontal lobe controls various behaviors, such as problem-solving, memory, language, spontaneity, judgment, impulse control, and social and sexual behavior. The neurotransmitter dopamine is a natural chemical in the brain's frontal lobe, and it is associated with reward and goal-driven behaviors. Your nervous system uses the dopamine to send messages between your nerve cells. It is a large factor in how we feel pleasure, think, plan, and focus.

It's important to have a parent or other adult to speak to when you put yourself in a risky or compromising situation. In this way, that trusted adult can walk you through the consequences of your actions to link that impulsive thinking or moment with facts instead of emotions. This type of interference can help the brain make the necessary connection in the future by wiring the brain to make that link the next time around. Surrounding yourself with positive role models can really help you along the way.

Pop Quiz

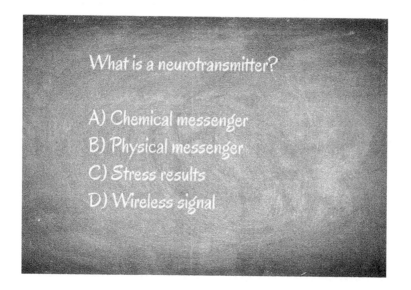

What is a neurotransmitter?

A) Chemical messenger
B) Physical messenger
C) Stress results
D) Wireless signal

Answer on page 197

The Company You Keep

You're probably familiar with the term "guilty by association." People judge you based on who you hang out with. Take an inventory of your friends. Are they the type of people your parents would be happy to meet? Do they share similar values, beliefs, or goals? How do they respond to pressure? Are they impulsive? Do they stretch or motivate you? Hindsight is 20/20; the people you associate with can have a significant impact on your personal success.

Be selective of your friends. Consider friends to play a different role in your life. We all need a friend who will party with us, but then drag us to study for exams or hold us accountable for finishing assignments. Choose friends that can be the voice of reason for you and others in the group. Seek diversity in your friendships. Your college has students from across the globe, don't just hang with those you know from across the street! It may take time to make life-long friends. Remember, friends come and go, and if you want quality friends, show yourself friendly, and the right people will be attracted to you.

Secure the Bag

Since most of us were never taught how to budget and manage money, college is a time to learn financial literacy. Consider join- ing different finance and other investment groups to teach you how to save, spend, and pay off your student loans. Money management will be an invaluable asset into adulthood. Trust me on this one.

CHAPTER 9

Balancing Act

There's something about the college experience that lets you know you had a guardian angel the entire time. Think about how many close calls you already had. Remember when your roommate passed out at that party? What about the time you were stranded in the hood with no means to get back to campus? The countless "almost" car accidents. And no one will tell your parents about the time you were shoplifting at Walmart. College life and risky behavior just go together.

Unprotected sex, binge drinking, and illegal drugs are rampant on college campuses. Why are students so reckless at this age? We talked earlier about the fact that the frontal lobe of your brain for rational decision-making is not fully developed until around age 25. Another problem is heightened peer pressure, so you are willing to go all out to impress others. Of course, I could tell you to be more disciplined and not engage in risky behavior, but that is not realistic. Everyone's doing it. But I will advise you to hang out with at least one other person, preferably in groups for safety.

UNHEALTHY BEHAVIORS: Substance Use And Abuse

Tobacco - Did you know that tobacco use is the leading cause of preventable death? Smoking often leads to lung cancer, respiratory disorders, heart disease, stroke, and other serious illnesses. CDC data indicates that cigarette smoking causes more than 480,000 deaths each year in the United States. Don't be fooled into thinking that e-cigarettes and vaping are safe alternatives. According to health experts, an e-cig- arette (i.e., Juul) contains as much nicotine as an entire cigarette pack in one cartridge. All of the products contain nicotine and

other chemicals. Unfortunately, these new smoking alternatives are marketed to high school and middle school students and offer candy and fruit flavors to entice them to buy. Knowing that cigarettes, e-ciga- rettes, and vaping contain addictive, dan- gerous chemicals should convince you to avoid them altogether.

Alcohol- Although alcohol is the go-to social ice-breaker, it is addictive and dangerous. Any party you go to on or off-campus is flowing with alcohol. Even younger people are drinking more alcohol than in the past. According to a 2018 National Survey on Drug Use and Health, 139.8 million Americans aged 12 or older drank alcohol with- in the past month, and 67.1 million people were binge drinkers.[9] Excessive alcohol consumption can increase your risk of stroke, liver cirrhosis, alcoholic hepatitis, cancer, and many other serious health conditions.

Another health risk caused by alcohol consumption is drinking and driving. This dangerous combination not only can lead to the loss of lives but as the driver, you will have a record of a DUI or DWI for at least five years and in most states ten years. Be smart. Be safe. You have nothing to prove to anyone. If you are going to drink, then drink in moderation.

In my conversations with the college student focus group, all of them have seen a variety of drugs on campus. A few smoked weed, others attend schools in states where weed is legal, so students openly smoke weed or eat weed edibles, in-between classes. It is impossible to cover the myriad of drugs on campuses today. For this guide, I want you to have an overview of the common drugs and their effects on your brain and body.

DRUGS

Cocaine - Cocaine, "coke" or "blow," is a potent stimulant that is snorted or inhaled as smoke (crack). It also dissolved and injected

into a vein. Cocaine is popular on college campuses and in society in general. Cocaine overdoses have increased in the past few years. Short term cocaine use can result in increased blood pressure, restlessness, and irritability. Long-term can result in serious medical issues such as heart attacks, seizures, and stomach pain. The bottom line, coke is a dangerous drug.

Hallucinogens

Hallucinogens are illegal drugs that alter your awareness, surroundings, thoughts, and feelings. These drugs are divided into two categories: classic hallucinogens (LSD) and dissociative drugs (PCP). Both of these types of drugs cause hallucinations which makes you feel that things are real when they are not — a dangerous disconnection from reality.[10] Hallucinogens are classified by the Drug Enforcement Agency (DEA) as a Schedule 1 Drug, which means that it has a high potential for abuse, with no currently accepted medical treatment.[11]

Hallucinogens are known to cause nausea, feeling relaxed or drowsy, paranoia, panic, hallucinations, and psychosis. An important thing to keep in mind is that hallucinogens interfere with the chemical serotonin in your brain, so it is altering a host of body functions.

*LSD has over 80 street names. The more common are Acid, Blotter, Dots, Trips, Mellow Yellow, and Window Pane.[12] It is considered one of the most potent, mood-changing chemicals. Most LSD is produced in crystal form and then converted into a liquid, capsules or gelatin squares. It is sometimes added to absorbent paper and sold in small squares decorated with cartoon characters and a variety of colors.

*Mushrooms or "shrooms" contain psilocybin, a naturally-occurring psychoactive and hallucinogenic compound. Psilocybin is a popular psychedelic, often called "Magic mushrooms" that can be dried and eat- en

overwhelmed

by mixing it into food or drinks. Magic

mushrooms are also known as shrooms, mushies, blue meanies, golden tops, liberty caps, philosopher's stones, and liberties, just to name a few. The altered state produced by shrooms is attractive to some students; however, this temporary state can become permanent in the brain and trigger a drug-induced psychosis.

Marijuana - So far, 11 states have legalized marijuana (cannabis) for recreational use. It has already been allowed for medical use in 47 states. There are conflicting sides as to the safety of marijuana, but the fact is that it impairs judgment and distorts perception in the short term and can lead to long-term memory impairment. The natural aspect of growing weed adds to the belief that it is safe. Marijuana edibles and CBD oil are extremely popular. The most important thing you need to know is that weed is a drug. Drugs are addictive. Drugs are harmful to your body.

Methamphetamines, also known as meth, blue, ice, and crystal, are powerful, highly addictive stimulants that affect your central nervous system. Meth users are prone to have mood swings, hallucinations, and paranoia. Meth can appear as a white, crystalline powder that dissolves in water or alcohol. Since 2011, meth overdose death rates have quadrupled.

Opioids- Opioids are powerful, dangerous drugs. Many people become addicted to them as painkillers. However, others inject heroin, which is highly addictive and life-threatening. More young people are overdosing on heroin around the country. In addition, injection of heroin increases your risk of contracting HIV (no cure, treatable with meds), Hepatitis B, and Hepatitis C (both can lead to liver damage).

Stimulants - Stimulants are a prescribed medication used to treat ADHD that works by changing natural substances in the brain.

overwhelmed

Stimulants are very popular on college

campuses because it can help increase your ability to pay attention, finish tasks, and improve listening skills. Contrary to popular belief, if the brain does not have a real attention deficit, then stimulants are not effective and can lead to addiction and even heart-related issues. Some widely-used brand names of stimulants include Adderall, Concerta, and Ritalin. Since these are controlled substances, there are knockoffs, so you really have no idea what you are ingesting to give you that energy boost. Extended use of stimulants decreases your need for sleep and loss of appetite. Too much of any drug is dangerous and can have negative health consequences in the long run.

As you transition into adulthood, both good and bad decision-making will follow you for the rest of your life. Don't waste your college dream experimenting with every drug or alcohol combination flowing around campus. There is *no* safe drug use. As a psychologist, I have witnessed first-hand how

casual drug use can permanently change the brain. Everyone thinks that it can't happen to them until it does. There is no way to predict if experimenting with drugs will forever alter your brain chemistry, and it isn't worth the risk. Spending the rest of your life in and out of psychiatric hospitals (which are very expensive) or drug rehab is not something that just happens to other people. It can happen to you.

Yes, you are overwhelmed and need an escape. Drugs and alcohol are not the answer. Try meditation, deep breathing exercises, working out, yoga, and therapy, to help you cope with everything that is going on inside and around you. You'll be happier and better off!

Question: How available are drugs on campus? Do you see students doing drugs at parties?

"In DC, weed is legal. Everyone smokes weed like it is a peppermint. They smoke before and after class. A lot of people smoke before their evening class. "

"Every party I have been to, there has been a lot of weed. Everyone is getting high. There are also a lot of weed edibles. All of my friends take Adderall to focus so they can finish their work."

"A lot of my friends are into psychedelics, and they are more popular. You can get shrooms just about everywhere on campus. I think shrooms are

popular because students think because they are from the earth, it is natural so nothing will

happen to them. Especially since they have been smoking weed for so long."

"At my school, there are a lot of harder drugs at parties and football games. Cocaine is very popular."

"When I was in high school, we were taking edibles and smoking weed for fun. After you keep doing it, it becomes part of your behavior. Weed is so normalized, and people start and have it in a fun way, and then they get addicted to the high, and before you know it, you are smoking four or five times a day. My friend has anxiety, and she smokes weed to calm down."

"Nobody I hang out with is into binge drinking or does heavy drugs. When we go to a party, we usually have one or two beers max. If we go to the club, we have one drink. I don't do drugs because I have no idea how it could affect my body, and I might end up doing something crazy!"

CONSENSUAL SEX

I know, everybody is having sex (at least it

seems that way)! It's a huge part of college

freedom if you are away from home. Sex is a topic that you are probably not comfortable talking about with your parents. Having a working knowledge of sexual relationships, sexual assault risk factors, and STD prevention can help you avoid these traumatic experiences in the future. Your sexual health and well-being should involve a mutually respectful approach to sexual relationships. And remember that it is perfectly fine and normal to abstain because soul ties and emotional attachments are actually "a thing."

Relationship Sex vs. Friends with Benefits

There is a stark difference between being in a relationship with someone versus casual sex. We often see characters on TV and in the movies involved in "friends with benefits" relationships. Although these types of hook-ups start out exciting, fun, with no-strings, they can lead to complications and heartbreak. One person may want

commitment, and the other wants to keep things the same. From a mental health perspective, relationship sex is better for your physical and emotional health when two people know each other well and care about each other.

Sexually Transmitted Disease

Sexually transmitted disease (STDs) is on the rise and is a health concern on college campuses. "Nearly half of the 20 million new STDs diagnosed each year are among young people aged 15–24 years. Women can have long term effects of these diseases, including pelvic inflammatory disease, infertility, tubal scarring, ectopic pregnancy, and chronic pelvic pain. About 1 in 4 (26 percent) of all new HIV infections are among youth ages 13 to 24 years. About 4 in 5 of these infections occur in males."[13] If you are sexually active, get tested every year for STDs, so that if you are diagnosed, you can get treatment and let your partner

know to get tested. As a rule of thumb, carry latex condoms when you go out, but be aware that using condoms consistently and correctly can reduce the risk of STDs, not eliminate them.

Sexual Relationship Tips

1. "Everybody is having sex" in college is a myth! Sexual relationships involve an emotional intensity that you may not be prepared to handle. Wait until you are ready.

2. Get to know the person before you rush into a sexual relationship. Trust and respect can ultimately lead to love.

3. Talk and agree about what is going to happen during sex. Get true verbal consent before having sex. It is OK to tell the other person that you want to stop in the middle.

Abusive Relationships

Intimate Partner Violence (IPV)

IPV is abuse or aggression that occurs in an intimate, close relationship. "Intimate partner" can be a current or former dating partner. IPV varies in duration and severity. It can range from one episode of violence that could have a lasting impact to chronic and severe episodes over multiple years. Intimate partner violence can occur in same-gender relationships.

Unfortunately, IPV is common and affects millions of people. IPV can start in adolescence, (Teen Dating Violence) and continues throughout a lifespan. According to the CDC's National Intimate Partner and Sexual Violence Survey:[14]

- About 1 in 4 women and nearly 1 in 10 men have experienced contact sexual violence, physical violence, or

overwhelmed

stalking by an intimate partner

during their lifetime and reported some form of IPV-related impact.

- Over 43 million women and 38 million men experienced psychological aggression by an intimate partner in their lifetime.

IPV includes four types of behavior:[15]

- **Physical violence** of hitting, kicking, or using another type of physical force to hurt the other partner.

- **Sexual violence** of forcing or attempting to force a partner to take part in a sex act, sexual touching, or a non-physical sexual event (e.g., sexting) when one partner does not consent.

- **Stalking** a partner that causes fear or concern for one's own safety or the safety of a third party close to the partner being stalked.

- **Psychological tactics** by using verbal and non-verbal communication intending to harm another person

mentally, emotionally, or exerting control over another person. Psychological tactics can often be difficult to identify.

In addition to the domestic violence tragedies of IPV survivors, there are also many adverse health outcomes resulting from IPV. Including conditions affecting the heart, digestive, reproductive, muscle and bones, and nervous systems, many of which are chronic. IPV survivors may experience mental health problems like depression and posttraumatic stress disorder (PTSD). Also, IPV survivors are at a greater risk of engaging in binge drinking and exhibiting risky sexual behaviors.

Warning Signs of a Controlling Partner

- You feel guilty when you are with your friends.

- They often talk about protecting you from others.

- They do not trust you and accuse you of cheating.

- They constantly criticize everything you do.

- They make you question your sanity, which means they are "gaslighting" you, causing you to question your judgment.

- They threaten to hurt themselves if you don't do what they want.

- They ask you to prove your love for them.

- They want your passwords and check your social media accounts.

Sexual Assault

Sexual assault is a common problem, but extremely serious on college campuses. It includes any unwanted sexual activity, from unwanted touching to rape. Regardless of age, race, or ethnicity, sexual assault is common among female students. In fact, one in five women in college experiences sexual assault.[16] The first few months of a student's first and second semester is the

highest risk of sexual assault. A challenge for college administration is that many students do not report sexual assault.

Statistics show that only one in five college-age women who are sexually assaulted report the attack to the police. More reporting can prevent attackers from hurting others and may help you feel more in control. Many sexual assaults on campus are the result of peer pressure and the need to fit in and participate in excessive partying, drinking, using drugs, or engaging in sexual activities that are not in your character. When you feel forced to engage in unwanted sexual activity for social acceptance, this is called sexual coercion. Listen to your inner voice. If someone is your true friend, they will not shame or criticize you for doing something against your core values. If you have been sexually assaulted, there are resources on campus and local and national organizations to help you, as well as

overwhelmed

information at the end of this book. Tell

someone you trust so they can support you through the process.

In today's social media and video environment, many people record events just to drive traffic to their page. Now more than ever, you cannot be a passive bystander and watch or record a sexual assault. I am not suggesting that you intervene in a manner that could be harmful, but I believe you are wise enough to use the technology at your fingertips or figure out a way to get help for the victim. Your act of intervention may save your fellow students' lives.

Sexual assault is not just a problem for women. Parents and school administrators should be talking about respecting boundaries early on so that by the time young adults are on their own, there will be no "gray area" about what assault is and what it isn't. You may want to check out the video, *Tea Consent (Clean)* on YouTube which describes consent in under three minutes and is worth discussing, more than once.[17]

IMPORTANT...

Rules for understanding true consent or informed consent based on sexual assault laws common in the United States and Canada are as follows[18]:

1. True consent requires that both people are emotionally and intellectually equal.

2. True consent requires honesty.

3. True consent requires understanding.

4. True consent requires permission to disagree or to refuse without penalty, harm, or ridicule.

5. True consent requires that both people really understand what is going to happen.

Minimize Risk of Sexual Assault

It is clear that sexual assault is not "caused" by particular behaviors, clothing, or any

other factors; however, there are ways to minimize the risk of being a target for sexual predators/perpetrators.

1. Avoid binge drinking. Alcohol is a factor in most campus sexual assaults.

2. When at a bar, do not accept a drink unless you have seen it poured by a bartender. Never leave your drink unattended.

3. Use a buddy system when going to a party. Buddies should never leave friends at a party.

4. Males especially should talk to each other about what true consent is and refrain from cosigning or ignoring rape culture. Real friends hold each other accountable.

IV: Who Am I?

CHAPTER 10

Unique

I think you will find it quite interesting to have a snapshot of the leading self-awareness theorists such as Sigmund Freud, Erik Erikson, Jean Piaget, and Kohlberg. This nutshell version of these theories will give you a better understanding of your behaviors since birth, up to this point in your college experience.

Sigmund Freud is known as the father of psychoanalysis. He was both a psychologist and physiologist with a degree in medicine. Freud is significant because he essentially explained early on that the mind and body are *not* separate. Hence, what is psychological is ultimately biological, and the reverse can also be true. This is known as conversion disorder. The functions of the ner-vous system may affect a person's physical movement, vision, or senses, which cannot be explained by a neurological disease or other medical condition. Conversion disorder symptoms are real and can cause significant stress or problems functioning.

In addition to giving us terms like a Freudian slip, Freud also helped explain the structure of the mind that seems to be most applicable to college students. He is known for the Id, Ego, and Superego psyche theories.[19] The Id is a person's drives and impulses. It deals with immediate gratification (food, sex, and comfort). The Ego is the source of our rational or reality-oriented functions. This is where we can decipher what is real, and we learn what is capable. Lastly, the Superego is where we derive our social, moral, and ethical restraints. Your Superego will kick in when someone commits a terrible act, and you say, "How could a person do that?"[20]

The next personality theorist is Erik Erikson. He created the Eight Stages of Psychosocial Development by building on Freud's Ego concept. Erikson's theory emphasizes

the rational and social capabilities. He believes that your development is only understood in the context of society and culture.[21] Any of your setbacks, challenges, or fears are based upon your cultural norms. Erikson assigns Eight Stages (we will only cover six) to your personality realization. Failure to master these tasks at the appropriate stage can lead to feelings of inadequacy.

Stage #1: Trust vs. Mistrust

Birth to 12 months old: Babies learn to trust adults to meet their basic needs for survival. Parents who respond to their baby's needs help the child develop a sense of trust so that the child views the environment as a safe, predictable space. On the flip side, if babies are not nurtured, they are likely to grow up with anxiety and mistrust people.

Stage #2 Autonomy vs. Shame/Doubt

Ages 1-3: Toddlers learn to explore their surroundings and act in their environ- ment to get results. They begin to discov- er their likes and dislikes as they relate to

food, clothing, and toys, as well as resolve the conflict of autonomy versus shame and doubt. This is what's called the "me do it" stage.

Stage #3 Initiative vs. Guilt

Ages 3-6: Preschoolers control their world through social interactions and play. Inter- acting with peers enables preschoolers to achieve their goals to master the task of ini- tiative and responsibility, which develops self-confidence. On the flip side, if a pre- schooler has overprotective parents, he or she may develop feelings of guilt.

Stage #4 Industry vs. Inferiority

Ages 6-12: Children begin comparing themselves to others. Children develop a sense of pride and accomplishment in their endeavors: academics, sports, social activities, and family. However, if a child concludes that he or she does not measure up, the child develops an inferiority complex that can last until adulthood.

Stage #5 Identity vs. Role Confusion

Ages 12-18: This age group struggles with "Who am I?" and "What do I want to do with my life?" At this adolescent stage, there is experimentation with different roles and ideas to see what fits best to journey into adulthood. Success at this stage offers a strong sense of identity to hold true to your beliefs. If you are confused at this stage, you will likely be confused as adults and struggle to "find" yourself.

Stage #6 Intimacy vs. Isolation

Ages 20-40: Once you develop a sense of

self, you are ready to share life with others. On the flip side, if you struggled with this at an earlier stage, you may have difficul- ty maintaining successful relationships and may experience loneliness and isolation.

The last expert in this personality area is Jean Piaget's four stages of cognitive devel- opment.[22] Piaget was the first psychologist to demonstrate the differences between how children think versus how adults think.

Sensorimotor stage: birth to 2 years - Children experience the world through reflex- es, senses, and motor responses;

Preoperational stage: ages 2 to 7 - Children learn a language and are egocentric and see things from their perspective;

Concrete operational stage: ages 7 to 11 - Children become more adept at using logic.

Formal operational stage: ages 12 and up - Children develop an increase in logical reasoning and think hypothetically. They also grow in moral, ethical, social, and phil- osophical reasoning.

Again, these are a few personality areas that you probably never thought about. Having an awareness of some of these frameworks can help you better understand yourself during this transition.

I also think you will find it interesting to learn about psychologist Lawrence Kohlberg's Moral Development Theory. Kohlberg creates three levels with six stages. For our nutshell, we are starting at Level 2:

Level 2

Stage 3: Ages 4-10 yrs - Conventional (Good boy/girl) - Children seek approv-al from others. They learn to abide by the rules and respond to their role when giv- en a task. Moral judgments are made based on the anticipated reward or punishment, "I'll probably get this positive reward if I do this," or "I'll probably get this negative re-port if I do that." At this stage children also conform to group expectations.

Level 3

Stage 5: Ages 11- adult - Post-convention-

al (Social contract, principled conscience) - You adopt a moral thinking pattern and consider the genuine interest of others. You identify what is right and wrong and form your individual principles or consciousness. Think of it this way, being honest, kind, and responsible has been ingrained in me, so now I have developed it for myself.

Morals are personal. They are formed based on your life experiences and your values and beliefs. Your morals give you the ability to judge between right and wrong. Let's face it, you know you should not lie, steal, cheat or hurt others. These are easy. It gets harder when the lie, in your mind, is "no big deal" or you cheat on just one or two answers or tests. Chances are your morals stemmed from your parents and as you get older, they become your own with a few tweaks. Regardless, you have to work hard to remain true to your values and beliefs at *all* times. It is not worth the embarrassment to yourself or your parents if you get kicked out of school.

On a broader level, morals and a moral code are contracts that you entered into through-out your education. You had to adhere to a student code of conduct that both and your parents signed in every school you attend-ed. Similarly, you signed a college code of conduct to indicate that you would follow the rules and adhere to moral and ethical

guidelines on campus. So, the idea that you are grown and can do whatever you want to do is false. Yes, you will probably get away with a few bad things, but it's not worth the risk. We are all held to an actual (school, work, career) contract and proverbial mor-al contract in society. Operating with high moral and ethical standards will serve you well now and in the future. At the end of the day, character counts!

Dr. Raushannah Johnson-Verwayne

RACE AND CULTURE

Cross's Black Racial Identity Development Model "Nigrescence" (Cross 1971, 1978, 1991)

Stage 1 Pre-Encounter	Desire to separate themselves from their racial group and assimilate and acculturate in the dominate society
Stage 2 Encounter	An awakening to racial consciousness due to experiences that calls race into perspective
Stage 3 Immersion/Emersion	Withdrawal from White culture and become immersed into Black culture
Stage 4 Internalization	A stable Black identity without having an anti-White perspective, being tolerant, more flexible, and rejecting racism and similar forms of oppression
Stage 5 Internalization-Commitment	Marked by social activism, social justice, and civil rights and a personal commitment to effecting change

Cross, W. E. (1971). The Negro to Black conversion experience: Toward a psychology of Black liberation. Black World, 20, 13-27.

Dr. Raushannah Johnson-Verwayne

Summary of Stages of Racial Identity Development

Integrated Model (John and Joy Hoffman)

CONFORMITY (Whites and People of Color): In the first stage of conformity, people of color and Whites feel that they are just "regular Americans." Unconsciously, members of both groups strive to emulate Whiteness in actions, speech, dress, beliefs and attitudes because Whiteness is perceived as positive.

People of Color

DISSONANCE: Dissonance for people of color occurs when they want to get along and be Americans but discover that their race or gender may preclude them from the benefits that Whites or males get. They start to feel confused about the beliefs they held about America and themselves as they begin to see that racism and sexism may be impacting them.

IMMERSION: These questions and disillusionment can lead to the immersion stage where women and persons of color feel angry about racism and sexism. They feel that most White people and males are racists and sexists and thus part of the problem. What might people of color do with this anger?

EMERSION: The fourth stage for people of color is emersion where their anger about racism directed towards Whites leads them to feel that they can only belong with others in their own racial group which understands them. They avoid, as much as possible, contacts with Whites and seek out people of their own race or gender.

INTERNALIZATION: Internalization occurs when they realize that there are negative qualities among their own people and that all White people are not the enemy. They see racism and sexism as the enemy and as something that they can fight against. They also manifest the desire to have more control over who they want to be. They are more than just a person of color or a woman

White People

ACCEPTANCE: In this stage, Whites can still dismiss or diminish comments or actions that indicate that racism is alive. They express the view that that everyone has struggles and people should just accept the way things are and try to be American. They expect of color to "get over it" and go forward as Americans which really means be more like White people.

RESISTANCE: Whites move from their acceptance stage to the resistance stage where they profess that racism is a thing of the past. Whites often express their belief that there is a new racism and that is the racism that they perceive is against Whites. This is popularly referred to as "reverse racism."

RETREAT: If their assumptions about people of color and their own lack of privilege are proven false, they may enter the retreat stage. They may feel guilty and ashamed by how hard life has been and still is for people of color. They are also frustrated by, annoyed, and impatient with other Whites who don't get it.

EMERGENCE: After feeling guilty and ashamed, Whites may move into the emergence stage where they start to understand their privilege and how it has and continue to benefit them. They also now begin to take control over the type of White person they want to be like.

INTEGRATIVE AWARENESS (both): In the last stage of integrative awareness, Hoffman asserts that Whites and people of color both come to the conclusion that there is much more to them than their race or gender. Both groups are able to positively identify with their own racial group while also acknowledging that other aspects of their identity (their gender, their talents and abilities, their unique experiences) contribute to their personhood.

4

CHAPTER 11

Black, White, And Brown

W hether you attend a local community college, midsize, or large university, you will encounter individuals from various cultures and races. Understanding and acknowledging the issues that racial identity plays into how you are perceived in society and how others perceive you will better prepare you for the real world. Taking time for self-reflection of your experiences, and learning to empathize with those who are not like you, will be advantageous. Several psychological frameworks describe the stages of racial and ethnic identity development that I believe will be useful. I will discuss a summary of the Stages of Racial Identity Framework[23] that focuses on the experiences of people of color (POC), biracial people (BP), and white

people (WP). Other cultural identity models can be found in the References.

Prejudice and Discrimination

As POC, we have borne prejudice and discrimination for hundreds of years. In 2020, we are at the height of the Black Lives Matter Movement (BLM) in our fight for racial equality and to end police brutality against Blacks. By now, you have probably experienced some form of individual discrimination in the way of microaggressions. Don't let the word "micro" fool you. The remarks or acts may seem harmless, but they can have a life-changing impact.

Microaggressions are the everyday, sub- tle, intentional, and often unintentional, interactions or behaviors that communicate some sort of bias toward historically marginalized groups.[24] For example, when a white person says to a POC, "Wow, you speak so well," or "That's a really nice outfit, did you get it on sale?" Then there are the nonverbal cues that POC regularly deals

with, such as being followed in a store, or a white woman clutching her purse when a Black man enters an elevator. All of these behaviors demonstrate racial bias.

Systemic/Institutional Racism

Often we hear people say that we need to "fix" the system that discriminates against POC or that the system is "broken." The reality is that the system was designed to work exactly as it has for years. It is the definition of systemic or institutional racism in which the government and other organizations developed systems to create and maintain racial inequality in almost every facet of life for POC. The disparities in access to wealth, justice, housing, employment, and education are prevalent. Get involved in student groups and organizations whose mission is to level the playing field for marginalized groups. Your thoughts and ideas are needed to flip the narrative. Change needs to happen legislatively and culturally to have a positive impact on your future.

First Gen

Are you a "First Generation" college student? A large number of POC and biracial students are First Gen. For our purposes, First Gen students are those whose par-ents did not earn a four-year college de-gree. The pressure to study for the SAT and ACT, complete FAFSA, and college appli-cations all by yourself is an overwhelming task. What many people don't realize is that First Gen students face unique challenges.

Statistics show that many First Gen students fail in higher education for social and economic reasons. Many First Gen students have excelled academically, yet a common factor these students share is a lack of knowl-edge about how college works and feel overwhelmed early on. One reason for this is that a lot of First Gen students never visit the campus before enrolling. So they have an uphill battle learning the ropes and are afraid to ask for help from professors and others.

First Gen students who are not enrolled in an HBCU have to continually deal with

microaggressions and racial prejudice from the "elitist" student body. These daily behaviors by others may make First Gen students feel isolated and result in low self-esteem. If you are a First Gen student, there are resources to help you navigate college listed at the end of this book. Don't be afraid to ask questions of your peers, professors, and academic advisors. Remember, you are the dream fulfilled. You've worked hard to get this far. Keep going. Graduation is within reach.

I spoke to a few First Generation college students to gain insight into their experiences. Not surprisingly, the similarities were uncanny in the summary of conversations.

Did you ever think you would go to college?

"I actually always dreamed of going to college even though my parents did not. I played basketball since I was a kid. The plan was to go to college on an athletic scholarship because there was no way my parents could afford it. It was stressful just applying because I didn't even have the money for the application fees, SAT, or ACT fees. I completed a lot of applications to get the fees waived. There was just a ton of paperwork to get into college, and my parents could not help

me. My parents were teenagers when they met. They were supportive of my dream, but they had no experience or even had friends who went to college to help me. I felt defeated early on because the kids in my school had trust funds and careers lined up if they finished college or not."

"College was something that no one in my family had done until I went and graduated. A part of me always wanted to go, but I wasn't sure if I had the grades or the stamina to make it. I literally had no help from guidance counselors, my

mom, or anyone. I found out what I needed to do on my own."

What was the hardest thing about college?

"For me, it was the culture shock. I went to a white high school because of basketball, but I lived in Atlanta. Going to college from Atlanta to Boston was crazy. There were no students who looked like me or talked like me. I felt like a total outsider. One girl I was friends with had two cars. That blew my mind. I didn't even know an adult back home who had two cars! I felt like there was no one I could relate to in any of my classes, so I pretty much kept to myself."

"The hardest thing for me was keeping up with the work. I did not have anyone to help me in the beginning. I was too embarrassed to get a tutor and ask for help until I was failing three classes. That's when I went to student support services and got a tutor. I was lucky because the tutor helped me do better with time management and set aside time slots to study. Trust me, so far, going to college and graduating is the hardest thing I have done by myself."

Did you experience any microaggressions or problems with professors, coaches, students?

"I'll be honest, of course, I felt the coaches were picking on me and much harder on me because I'm the Black girl. Deep down, I knew they expected me to be the most athletic and tougher than my teammates. It was like the stereotypical Black student-athlete. I just shut down a lot because I did not know how to deal with the coaches or navigate the situation.

Then in my Professional Ethics class, it was the biggest eye-opener when the professor had the entire class do the "Privilege Walk." Basically, *you move forward if you've had some advantage that the professor named, and you take a step backward if you had some disadvantage that was called. At the end of the walk, I was one of two people against the wall **facing backward**. This experience gave me a perspective that was, yeah, I am up against the wall, but since we are all in the same room, I had to do everything in my power to make it out and finish college, at least to the point that I was facing forward."*

"I remember my laptop crashed, and I could not afford a new one. I was sleeping in the library to use the computer because I knew that I had to get through the semester and be able to buy one with my summer job. One night I was in the library, and there was a power outage. I almost cried.

A white student nearby said, "You can just finish it in your room."

I replied, "My laptop died."

"So, why don't you just get a new one?"

Her remark made me want to cry harder, but I could not give her that satisfaction or tell her that there was no way I could afford a laptop. I took a deep breath and said, "Yeah, I never thought of that!"

She walked away with this incredulous look on her face like I was from another planet.

What advice do you have for First-Generation college students?

"The biggest piece of advice I can give to first- gen students is to advocate for themselves. No

one is going to be looking out for you like they did in high school. If you feel like you deserved an A- or an A+ on a paper? Talk to the professor. Ask questions. Ask why. I was lucky that I knew I could talk to professors about grades and performance; these aren't set in stone. Flunk a test, talk to that professor, and make an effort. Show that you're trying, and they'll benefit you the most they can. Don't assume that they'll see your grades flunking and try to reach out to you. Some will, but you need to be the one out there and asking questions.

Also, take care of yourself. I knew my family was my biggest support network, so moving to Boston and being mostly alone made me almost im-

mediately rely on myself. It's okay to ask for help. It's okay to fall down. Don't think that being a first-gen student means you have to perform perfectly. We're all learning together, and stumbling is part of the process. Know what your limits are, and know when to tap out."

"I had no idea about the importance of networking and internships. I totally missed out

on internship opportunities, which could have landed me a job in my field. I had friends, but I did not look to them as a networking opportunity after college. I really liked some professors, but I never went to them for a referral or recommendation. I did not know the importance of building my resume to build relationships. Another piece of advice is to ask for help, ask questions from students and professors. You are really not supposed to know everything."

CHAPTER 12

Self-Identity

I've heard people say, "I just need to find myself!" Sometimes we say things like this to avoid dealing with a challenging situation. We all need to step back and take an honest evaluation of ourselves. To become self-aware means you have a keen awareness of your one and only unique self; you know what makes you happy, sad, emotional, angry, or fulfilled. Basically, knowing your key triggers will allow you to handle situations better.

Take an honest self-evaluation of your personality, including your strengths, weaknesses, thoughts, beliefs, motivation, and emotions. This will also help you become more in tune with how others perceive you. Every encounter that you have, whether good, bad, or indifferent, your mind will give you an interpretation of that experience for the future and creates a pattern for handling it going forward. The more aware you are of your actions and attitudes in certain interactions you will be able to change bad behaviors for better ones.

One important point I want to make is that people often use the terms self-awareness and purpose interchangeably. A quick Google search for "finding your purpose" will yield over one billion books. Why? Because so many people need help figuring out what they were put on this Earth to do. Your purpose is where you discover the meaning of *why* you desire to do what you do—your drive, your passion. On the other hand, becoming self-aware gives you a deeper understanding of your personality, so it should be the first step in the soul-searching process which will ultimately lead you to your purpose.

Gender Identity

Gender identity is your sense of being male or female. Some people feel that their gender identity, how they really feel about themselves, is different from their physical bodies. For example females may feel like males or vice versa. Still, you may encounter others who do not identify with either gender. For those who feel that their gender identity is different from their assignment at birth are described as transgender.

LBGTQIA

Learning who you are and what makes you tick can be difficult. It can be more challenging when you also have to deal with other people's perception of you. College life is stressful and it poses added stress for students who identify as LGBTQIA (Lesbian, Gay, Bisexual, Transgender, Queer, Questioning, Intersexual, and Asexual). Many LGBTQIA students face discrimination and pressure from their families or communities, which may put them at greater risk for emotional health struggles.

All students need to feel valued and supported. If you have a friend who identifies as LGBTQIA, be there for them as best you can. Do not be judgmental. Do your best to listen and empathize as well as ed- ucate yourself about what they are going through. Encourage your friend to seek support from the school resource center if they are struggling emotionally.

"Be yourself. Everyone else is already taken."

–Oscar Wilde

V: Learning to Cope

CHAPTER 13

Mindfulness

Your words matter. Those thoughts roaming around in your head that flow through your mouth determine your emotions and mood. How often do you talk to yourself? Do you speak words of encouragement or defeat? Self-talk can influence how you feel about yourself and how you respond to life's daily challenges. Your self-talk is the words you use to frame your life. If you speak negative messages to yourself, your brain will develop automatic thoughts and take you to a negative emotional reaction. By the same token, if you practice positive self-talk, you actually feel better about yourself and your outlook for the day.

"You can't control what happens to you in life but you can control how

overwhelmed

you react to it."

Positive self-talk is a skill. We naturally talk to ourselves all the time, but we have to make sure that what we are saying is productive and empowering. Positive self-talk is supportive and affirming and should be in the first person and use the word "I" to speak in the first person. Here are a few examples:

- "I'll raise my hand in biology today because I am really confident about the central nervous system."

- "I like how I look in this outfit. I will dress like this more often."

Be mindful of your self-talk. Is it positive or negative? Consider writing down your self-talk to see if there are patterns. Work on changing the dialogue of your negative self-talk patterns.

Coping Skills

There is a type of Cognitive Behavioral

Therapy (CBT) developed by Marsha Linehan, called Dialectical Behavioral Therapy

(DBT). I know this is getting a little technical, but stay with me. DBT effectively treats a variety of disorders, including depression, substance abuse, eating disorders, and PTSD. I will touch upon other DBT modules that will help reduce your overwhelmed triggers in the next two chapters.

The first part of the DBT Module involves Mindfulness. Learning to be mindful, by focusing and breathing property will help you utilize the other modules effectively to cope and reduce your stress.

The Three States of Mind

1) **Logical Mind** (also known as the reasonable mind) is just like it sounds. A person uses their logical mind when they consider only the facts.

2) **Emotional Mind** is the atten- tion-seeker of the three states of mind. A person uses their emotion- al mind when only feelings control thoughts

overwhelmed

and behavior. They may act

impulsively and think about the consequences later.

3) **Wise Mind** is the balance of the two.
The wise mind considers both log- ic
and emotion to control thoughts and
behaviors. People use their wise mind
when they use the word "and"
instead of "but" in decision-making.
Balance is the key.

When practicing Mindfulness (your Wise-
Mind), your goal is to observe the situation,
describe it, and participate in it. In doing so,
you must be open-minded, non-judgmen-
tal, and effective in your decision-making.
Again, this takes practice. If you feel mindfulness is not working, then try to remember the IMPROVE acronym to help you get
back on track.

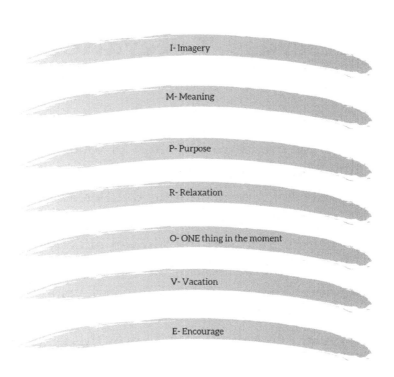

I- Imagery

M- Meaning

P- Purpose

R- Relaxation

O- ONE thing in the moment

V- Vacation

E- Encourage

Challenge: Try to use "and" instead of "but" when problem-solving or communicating. For example, instead of "I love you but you make me angry" try saying "I love you and you make me angry at times." Use "and" in a variety of problem-solving situations.

CHAPTER 14

Distress Tolerance

Overwhelming feelings in response to the pressures and stress of college life is something that all students face regardless of their academic abilities. Learning how to communicate and manage your emotions to lessen the burden effectively can help. There is a type of Cognitive Behavioral Therapy (CBT) that was developed by Marsha Linehan, called Dialectical Behavioral Therapy (DBT). I know this is getting a little technical, but stay with me. DBT is effective in treating a variety of disorders, including depression, substance abuse, eating disorders, and PTSD.

I want to provide you with a nutshell of the skills needed to achieve less stressful outcomes: mindfulness, distress tolerance, and emotion regulation. Mindfulness is to be fully aware and present in the moment. Our minds naturally drift into other areas, but when we practice mindfulness techniques, we can get back on track. Mindfulness can be done sitting, standing, walking, or lying down. It is taking a moment to pause, meditate, and incorporate another activity like yoga or exercise.

Distress tolerance is your ability to manage your internal emotional state in response to stress-inducing factors. If you have a low distress tolerance, you will be quick to react negatively to mildly stressful situations. DBT can help you in this area. In the past, treatment focused on avoiding stressful situations, which makes sense, but is easier said than done. Today, you can embrace those stressful situations and learn how to engage with them appropriately. The key aspect of distress tolerance is awareness of your emotional state. You can learn to calm your body down with self-soothing activities like controlled breathing, meditation, yoga, and progressive muscle relaxation.

Pain is an unavoidable part of life, but suffering is unnatural. There is no doubt that you will encounter some uncertain and challenging times. There are many quotes about overcoming adversity, but one of my favorites is Frederick Douglass, "With- out struggle, there is no progress." What I would add is that one must be *both* intentional and skillful in overcoming adversity. It doesn't happen automatically. Resilience is an action word.

It is also super important to understand your emotions. I always ask clients, "how does that make you feel?" I've found that even those with extensive and impressive vocabularies often struggle with this question. Emotions are layered. For example, "mad" might actually be "hurt" or "abandoned" and happy could be "proud" or "resolved." The better you understand your feelings, the easier it will be to communicate your needs and expectations to others. Spend some time exploring the **Feelings**

Wheel.

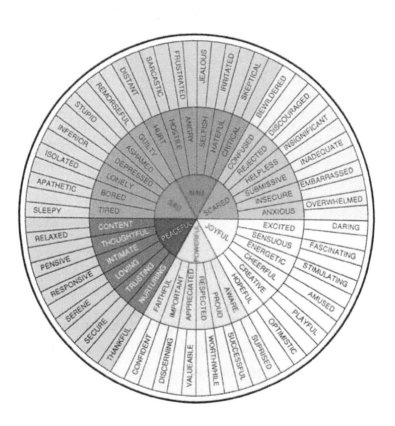

CHAPTER 15

Emotion Regulation

Emotional or self-regulation requires you to deal with both positive and

negative feelings, to help you learn how to strengthen, use, and control them. There are three components to this communication therapy:

- Initiating actions triggered by emotions.

- Inhibiting actions triggered by emotions.

- Modulating responses triggered by emotions.

Studies show that the average person has 12,000 to 60,000 thoughts per day, and 80% of those thoughts are negative, and 95% were the repetitive thoughts from the previous day.[25] Our thoughts create emotion-provoking stimuli that require some type of action or response. Practicing emotional regulation acts as a modifier to fil- ter only the important information so that we can handle it in a way that does not in- voke stress. When we are provoked, our brain automatically goes into fight or flight mode. By practicing emotional regulation, we can learn to "buy time" before we react and ultimately have a better balance of our feelings and actions.

Emotional Regulation

* When faced with a stressful event, pause for a moment to objectively assess the situation. This will give you a better chance to

react more calmly.

* A cool head will likely help you remain true to your core values rather than deviate and act impulsively, which you may later regret. Try these skills to help you stay calm during those challenging moments:

- **Self-awareness check** - Express your emotions and feelings. If you can write them down;

- **Mindful awareness check** - Try a breathing exercise or sensory relaxation to help you get to a calm state;

- **Cognitive reappraisal** - Pause and try to look at the situation from another perspective. For example, "The professor hates me!" You can reappraise that thought with "I know I haven't given this class a full effort. I am a lot better than this. I will apologize for my lack of effort and do better."

- **Objectively adapt** - Instead of viewing your stressful situation from your perspective, think of how your mom or a close friend would react or handle the situation.

- **Me time** - Get into the habit of a self-care routine that includes adequate sleep, meditation, repeating positive affirmations, journaling, and breath relaxation.

Frequently check on your thoughts to see if they need an upgrade. Thoughts lead to behaviors, behaviors lead to habits, and habits create your life, and more important- ly, habits can define your future. Redefine failure and train your brain to be mentally strong. It all starts with a single thought.

"YOU HAVE THE POWER TO DECIDE
IF YOU WILL IMPULSIVELY REACT
OR INTENTIONALLY RESPOND."
-DR. RJ

CHAPTER 16

Interpersonal Effectiveness

In high school, you had to remember a lot of facts and other information to pass your exams and the standardized tests. Now that you are in college, you proba-bly came up with several acronyms to jog your memory. Another prong to the DBT communication strategy is interpersonal effectiveness. Using the "DEAR MAN" skill and acronym will help you develop asser-tiveness and get what you want out of your relationships. The "DEAR MAN" skill will teach you how to respond to situations in a nonjudgmental way.

D= Describe

Describe what you want clearly to avoid misunderstandings. Never assume the other person knows what you mean.

E= Express

Express your feelings and opinions about the situation. Pay attention to your tone and body language to show you mean business. Never assume the other person knows how you feel.

A= Assert

Assert yourself and ask for what you want or say no calmly and politely. Never assume that others are going to do what you want voluntarily — you have to speak up and ask.

R= Reinforce

Reinforce or reward the person early on and relay the potential for a positive outcome. The point here is that the person should want to do what you asked and not feel like they have to do it.

M= Mindful

Maintain your firm position, and don't be distracted or waiver. Practice mindfulness if the other person becomes hostile or defensive.

A= Appear Confident

Appear effective and competent. Make eye contact and keep the appropriate tone.

N= Negotiate

You must be willing to give to get. Compromise is the rule of thumb. Respect that the other person has limits as well.

Now that you have the DEAR MAN skill for communicating effectively, you may also want to add the GIVE FAST acronym to this process. GIVE will teach you how to respect the other person's thoughts and feelings. FAST will teach you how to respect yourself in the process.

G= Gentle

Be gentle, even if you are mad at the person.

I= Interested

Let the person know that you are interested in what they have to say. You can nod or make eye contact or even repeat what you heard.

V= Validate

Validate the other person's thoughts or feelings.

E= Easy Manner

Make the conversation natural and easy. Pay attention to your body language, tone, and smile.

F= Fair

Be fair in your negotiations.

A= Apologies

If you disagree with the person's viewpoint, do not apologize if it goes against your values.

S= Stick to values

Be true to your values and beliefs.

T= Truthful

Be truthful and strive for authenticity and honesty.

Self-Care

Make sure there is a self-care routine in your schedule, even if it's only five or ten minutes of meditation or deep breathing exercises. It's important to take time for yourself.

Self-care is essential for survival through college and beyond.

Self-care requires deliberate acts to ensure that your mental, emotional and physical health are in check.

"FUEL YOUR MIND, BODY AND SPIRIT. YOUR COLLEGE JOURNEY IS A MARATHON NOT A SPRINT." -DR. RJ

VI: Reach Out

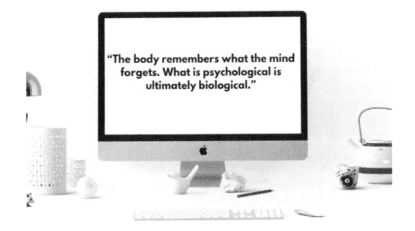

"The body remembers what the mind forgets. What is psychological is ultimately biological."

CHAPTER 17

Safe Space

U nfortunately, stigma and shame have prevented many Black people from seeking help from a licensed therapist. Therapy is not "paying someone just to talk." It is a scientifically-proven process that teaches you about the inner workings of your mind. Still, it also helps you manage your emotions, reconstruct better behaviors, and manage your thoughts in a healthier way. The goal is so that you can live happier and balanced. Many therapists use Cognitive Behavioral Therapy (CBT), which helps you set goals, track progress, and measure results. CBT enables you to build emotional resilience so that you can end therapy and manage on your own. Take control of your life and try therapy. It's definitely a priceless investment in your

overwhelmed

overall self-care and wellness routine.

You'd be surprised by the things people say to me about why they choose *not* to engage in therapy:

"What happens in my house stays in my house. I wasn't raised to be telling all my business!"

"Some stuff you just need to figure out on your own."

"Therapy is for crazy, rich, white, weak people."

"I can't afford it."

"I don't have time."

"There's nothing wrong with me."

"I don't see how talking about something over and over will help."

"I just pray and fast."

"My pastor said that depression is a sin."

"I tried it once, and it just made me feel

worse."

"Talking about all that stuff made me feel worse, it was better when I pretended nothing happened."

"I'm not paying people to listen to my problems."

Many people, regardless of ethnicity, feel the same way, but these responses are just not accurate. These common misconceptions prevent people from making positive, life-changing benefits for themselves and those around them. Although the importance of mental health awareness is trending on social media, more needs to be done on college campuses to provide accurate information on the advantages of engaging in therapy and the various forms. Regardless of whether you believe you have a big issue or a small issue, a therapist can help. The worst part about this is that all it takes is for one person to have a bad experience, and then *all* therapeutic approaches are painted with a negative brushstrok

Question: Are you aware of the mental health resources at your school? Have you used them?

"To be honest, I remember a flier during Freshman Week that said students have free mental health visits. I don't even know where the building is! I have not seen it, and I do not know anyone who has used it."

"At my school, the administration promoted mental health a lot, so I used it. I don't think it was helpful for me. The counselors specialize in certain areas, and when it came time to match me with the right counselor, I just don't think I had a match at all. The counselor did not help me or offer suggestions to help with my issue. If anything, the counselor was boring and did not show empathy as a counselor. I expected more."

"In my school, I don't know where my counselor is located. I have an advisor, but I have been given a different person each time. The administration is not good in this area. Having a mental health counselor is not on the list of priorities for my school."

IS MEDICATION FOR ME?

People of color often have a cultural mistrust of medicine, doctors, psychologists, and social workers for valid reasons. Historically, systematic racism has contributed to deadly experimentation like the Tuskegee Syphilis Study, misdiagnosis of learning and behavioral disorders, separation of families (foster care), and several other injustices. However, complete mistrust can lead to ineffective treatment and unnecessary suffering.

Check out the guidelines below to help you make an informed decision. The best treatment includes collaboration between you,

your primary care physician, your therapist, and a psychologist.

➢ Share your symptoms with all of your
providers. I often find that my patients
have shared symptoms with me that
their PCP is unaware of, such as
insomnia or gastrointestinal issues.

➢ Get an updated physical often. Hormonal imbalances, thyroid issues, or
other medical conditions come with
anxiety and depression symptoms.

➢ SLEEP! Lack of sleep wreaks havoc on
the brain and the body.

➢ Eliminate avoidable stress and add
"relaxation" to your To-do list.

➢ Manage your response to stressors.

➢ Chronic stress can kill!

➢ Improve your diet. Excessive sug- ar,
fatty foods, processed foods, and junk
food can alter your mood and energy
level.

➢ Do your own research. Use reputable resources and ask questions.

➢ Build a relationship with your practitioners. You are the expert of you, and we are on your team.

➢ Remember that medication is not a cure. It treats symptoms. Wellness is achieved by a daily and consis- tent routine of self-care. The mind, body, and spirit must *all* be healthy to achieve wellness.

HOW TO CHOOSE A THERAPIST

• Ask friends and family for referrals.

• Research online: psychologytoday. com and review photos and profiles. Therapyforblackgirls.com is a national network of culturally informed therapists.

• Be sure that your therapist is licensed in your state.

- Find a therapist who specializes in your area of concern.

- Ask if your therapist has a therapist or has been in therapy. I personally would not want a therapist who hasn't been in therapy before.

- Interview your therapist. Most therapists allow a brief complimentary phone consultation.

- Hang in there. Don't give up after a few sessions. However, if your therapist truly isn't a good fit, let her know and ask for a referral.

CHAPTER 18

What's Next?

If there's one thing that students, parents, and college administrators agree on, is that the transition from high school to college is an emotionally overwhelming and stressful time for students. Most students are worried about socializing and academics, without realizing that their stress and anxiety could lead to mental health issues or risky behaviors. Parents are concerned about the college search and finances. The colleges and universities are concerned about tuition being paid.

The entire structure of the high school experience and college experience are vastly different. For example, high school attendance is mandatory. College attendance is voluntary. Being mentally prepared for such freedom is a big deal. The majority

of high school students have not learned how to make good choices. There is a lot more hand-holding and encouragement in high school than in college. Professors are not going to remind you to hand in assignments or tell you to study for tests. Most high school work is reading, memorizing, and discussing in class. In college, the syllabus has a ton of reading assignments that you will never discuss.

Parents, your child needs you to help them navigate through the college wilderness. Make it a priority to know all the types of academic and mental health resources your student's school offers. Be proactive. Let them know that you are cheering for them in the nosebleeds. Neither of you will ever get this time back, so work together to make it less painful and even enjoyable.

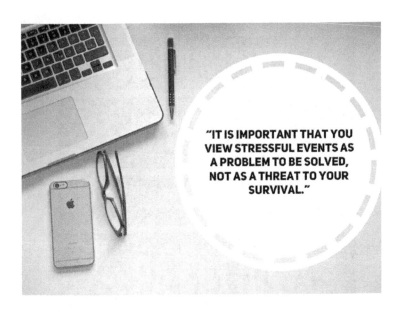

"IT IS IMPORTANT THAT YOU VIEW STRESSFUL EVENTS AS A PROBLEM TO BE SOLVED, NOT AS A THREAT TO YOUR SURVIVAL."

VII: College Roundtable

CHAPTER 19

Parents Speak

I spoke to several parents who have kids in college who are sophomores, juniors, and seniors at colleges primarily in the Southeast, U.S. Below are a few of their responses to common, yet critical questions and decisions that parents make as they send their kids out into the real world.

My Mom Said

Question: What worries you the most about college and your kids?:

"Access to drugs, alcohol, promiscuity, and them being able to handle all of that and maintain a proper education."

"Access to upperclassman and not being mature enough to handle that in terms of date rape,

heartbreak, and upperclassman guys."

"I am wondering if they talk about consent and sex in college. That's important, but I am not sure anyone wants to talk about it honestly."

Question: Would you buy a book about self-care for your college student?:

"I would because I want to know for sure what they are going through and what signs to look out for."

"I think I would buy it as well, but I believe there is a difference in whether your child attends an HBCU or PWI. From a PWI standpoint, you are expected to just go to class, and there is a lot less social pressure to fit in. At an HBCU, everyone is trying to be this popular person and the next IG famous. Girls must have the perfect outfit, hair, nails, flawless makeup, and lashes just to go to class. It is a lot different than when I went to college. We just threw on jeans and a sweatshirt and pulled our hair in a bun."

"I think at a PWI, you can be invisible. At an

HBCU, you are seen, and someone is checking

*for you. You have to start early and figure out
what you want to be and how you want to be
perceived. What you want to wear and how far
you want to take that is important. Party clothes
are not for class. Your reputation is important.
You have to be able to be smart and know how to
have a good time within reason."*

*"A guidebook is a good start because it is a lot for
them to figure out. Going to the party, what to
wear, what to drink, what to eat, what time to
leave to be up for class. The freedom can be a lot
for kids to figure out in a short amount of time."*

**Question: What types of discussions did
you have with your college-bound kid before they left?**

*"I talked to my daughter about suicide, depres-
sion, drugs, and sex. We talked about guys because I think my daughter is guy-crazy. I tried
to keep it lighter and not a lecture."*

*"I did not have long talks about drugs and al-
cohol because we spent a lot of time on those*

subjects in high school. We also discussed suicide and depression when my son was in high school."

"I talked to my daughter, mostly about boys and sex. Let's be honest; I don't want her to get pregnant in college. I'm not saying it's the end of the world, but it would require a change of plans, focus, and responsibilities."

"I just wanted my son to know that he is going to be under stress in general, so don't get too stressed out about grades. I just want him to finish."

"I gave my son a box of condoms. Boys' hormones are raging on college campuses. I want him to be responsible and, most of all, respectful. I don't recall having a talk with him about drugs, depression, or suicide. My kids know people who have committed suicide, so that did not cross my mind."

"I was not too worried about drugs or alcohol. The thing I was worried about and even scared about was the boys. I had many conversations with my sister circle on how to help my daughter deal with the onset of grown men. When she got *on campus, she was the hottest thing, and I did not know how to help her. I was not that hot in college!"*

Question: What advice do you have for parents with kids going to college now?

"I would tell parents to keep lines of communication open and judgment-free. Their kids will experience people and things they have never experienced in their shelteredworld."

"Remind their kids to be careful who they hang around because they can easily become that person. People remember you by your group of friends. Take it slow. Four years go by fast, and people don't forget what you did freshman year."

"I agree that communication is the hardest part. Parenting an adult is harder than when they were younger, and you told them what to do. Now, all you can do is listen since they already made their choice. Try to sprinkle the advice and not be too preachy."

"I would tell parents not to push what they did onto their child. You have to let them figure out

who they are and what they are capable of in certain situations."

"Parents have to learn how to transition from being a parent to a friend. Friends are open and honest with each other."

Question: If your college student was clinically depressed, would they know what to do?

"I don't think so. Mental health is not something we talk about often, and when we do, it is more about not stressing over small things and finding time to relax."

"I think I was fortunate because my son confided in his roommate, and his roommate suggested he seek counseling. I believe that my disconnect was differentiating between growing up and high school stuff versus actually being clinically depressed."

"My daughter and I talked about depression, and she said that if she thought she needed therapy, she would not come to me first because she would not want me to know that she needs help. I guess I should be OK with the fact that she recognizes

that there is help available."

Question: What does a successful college career look like for your child? Does it match yours?

"I am not pressuring my child to finish with a 4.0 and get a job at a Fortune 500 company. I really just hope she does well and enjoys the experience."

"This is my son's second school. He failed out before. Now he has matured and is getting A's and B's, so he is really happy with himself. I keep telling him that it is more important to finish something you started."

"I think deep down we want our kids to follow in our footsteps or at least do things that we did, especially if we are successful. I have tried not to interfere or convince her to go a certain route to achieve her goals. Ultimately she will figure out the best path for herself."

Dr. Raushannah Johnson-Verwayne

A Message to Parents:

Congratulations on helping your child reach a

major life milestone. I imagine that you sit back and reminisce how time has flown by, and your precious baby is now an adult. Al- though you worried about your child through- out their elementary and high school years, you had control of their whereabouts. You had rules that they had to follow. Now, they are off into the "wilderness" for lack of a better word, to live independently, gain knowledge to em- bark upon a fruitful career, and hopefully not embarrass you.

*I'm not sure if you realize it, but when your child leaves home for college, it is actually a loss. Each one of us grieves and handles loss differently. On the outside, you may be cheering and telling others that you're partying like a rockstar. Yet on the inside, you are sad, afraid, and racked with worry. I think most of the concern is because you remember the things that **you** did as a college student; all of the close calls that could have been tragic. Unfortunately, there is not much you can do but let go and trust that your child will*

overcome the "wilderness" like you did, even if

there are a few bumps and bruises.

In reality, you are your child's biggest role model. Of course, their friends are important, but they have watched you up close and from afar. How you have carried yourself and responsibilities as a parent will profoundly impact them during this transition and in the future. Even though they are grown and doing God knows what on campus, here are a few things that the college students in my focus group suggested you could do to help them get through this period:

* ***Check-in*** - Your college student may say or even think they can get through this transition without your involvement, but they need to know that you are still a phone call or text away. Frequent communication will make both of you feel more connected despite the distance.

* ***Listen*** - Your college student wants to open up with you and share their thoughts, feelings, experiences, and

* opinions. This is your time to listen and

not lecture or become judgmen- tal. Offer advice, but let them know that the ultimate decision is theirs.

* *Let go* - Now is the time to get rid of any preconceived notions of what your child's college life should look like. Keep in mind that times have changed, and it may look a lot differ- ent than yours. Again, hold off on the lectures and judgment. Try to relax and enjoy the stories and moments with them in their world.

* *A Few Free Passes* - Your college stu- dent is already stressed and over- whelmed with new responsibilities. Don't be too hard on them for fail- ing an exam, breaking a campus rule, or making a bad choice. Your child is not perfect—neither are you. Re- member what you did in college ☺. Be more tolerant than in the past. Your child will open up to you more

about serious issues like their mental health,

drugs, alcohol, or sex.

As parents, you can help by allowing your children to make mistakes along the way and resist the urge to rescue, starting by gradually increasing responsibilities and independence as early as third grade. Parents can also encourage their children to advocate for themselves in middle school and high school. Many adolescents begin college with no practice of basic college survival skills and subsequently panic when a situation arises.

Keep in mind that the idea of perfection also sabotages students. Research suggests that over time, perfectionism has increased partially due to the latch-key kid generation growing up to become helicopter parents. This is in response to the subtle and sometimes obvious neglect of their own childhood. Think about the generation of children born in the no seatbelt, smoking in cars, no help with homework, and home alone. Now they have their own children, and they recall their feelings of fear, which was not acceptable

to express at that time because neglect was a cul-

tural norm. If you are an 80's baby, you can like-ly recall situations where you vowed that when you grew up, you would never let this happen to your child, and there lies the origin of the ex-treme perfectionist. Now, you raise your children under a microscope and inadvertently shape to-day's overachiever. What do you think of when you hear the term perfectionist? It's not rigid or predictable, order, or even success. However, the underlying reason for perfectionist tendencies includes an intense fear of failure, the need for approval, and subconscious shame. Unchecked perfectionism can have serious emotional conse-quences that lead to anxiety, depression, suicidal thoughts, and a host of addictions.

Perfectionists are often praised because of their ability to get things accomplished, and their de-structive behavior goes unnoticed. Yet they have this inherent belief that they are not good enough unless they meet these rigid standards for success. Perfectionism comes with an inner constant critic over responsibility and discounting painful emo-tions or past trauma. Perfectionists are always

there for others, but share very little of who they

really are and what problems they might have. Being a perfectionist can be a lonely place. If this is you as a parent, it is OK to talk to a professional about your pain and discuss subtle ways to decrease the volume of your shameful inner self-critic voice. If you know someone who is a perfectionist, praise them for who they are, not for tangible things or accomplishments. Release your expectations of them and make room for them to be comfortable with practicality and normalcy.

Take heart in knowing that you did the best you could to prepare a well-rounded adult. It's up to your child to run with this opportunity and make the most of it. In the grand scheme of life, all will be well. Finally, please don't convert your child's bedroom into your yoga studio just yet! Ah, life 101, to be continued...

A Message to Counselors:

As mental health professionals, we have to do a better job addressing the emotional and behavioral challenges of the college students enrolled in our schools. Since we already know that more than half of college kids suffer from depression, anxiety, or stress, and on nearly every college campus, there are limited resources and education about mental health issues.

From a resource perspective, we know that there are not enough paid mental health professionals to support a fraction of the student body. I spoke to a distraught student after being turned away from the counseling center because she did not have an appointment. What should she have done in the meantime? What if this resulted in a tragedy? We have to do better.

I have spoken to several college students, and all of them are aware that they have academic advisors and can access student health services, but they rarely use them. Many students feel that the counselors do not understand them as some of the counselors are either older than their parents or seem like students themselves. From a diversity perspective, students of color do not feel that white counselors can empathize with them. More importantly, the trust factor is gone. Staff and others around campus discuss student challenges as if it were a gossip session. This is extremely unprofessional.

Here are a few things that I believe we could do to better support the student body:

* Establish a course platform around mental illness

* Increase access to mental health services

* Create a better system

* Peer counseling

* Community forums and initiatives

As Counselors, you can also change the narrative of failure by encouraging resilience and pointing out cognitive distortions (i.e., catastrophizing, black and white thinking). You can also display quotes about resilience in your offices, on your webpages, and on social media. Of course, there is a lot of work to do, but we must begin the dialogue and take action to help students during one of the most important milestones in their lives.

D r. Raushannah Johnson-Verwayne, also known as "Dr. RJ" is a licensed clinical psychologist and the founder of Standard of Care Psychological Services, LLC, in Atlanta, GA. Dr. RJ brings a balance of science, practicality, wit, humor, and re-latedness to the clinical field. Dr. RJ focuses on the assessment and treatment of com-mon disorders such as depression, anxiety and trauma. She integrates education of the brain and body connection and explains neuroscience in a relatable manner. Dr. RJ empowers clients to gain a full understand-ing of their condition in order to produce long-lasting changes in health and overall well-being beyond their time in treatment.

RAUSHANNAH JOHNSON-VERWAYNE

Dr. Raushannah Johnson-Verwayne

Dr. RJ is a proud alumna of North Carolina A&T State University and earned her doctorate degree in Clinical Psychology from the Georgia School of Professional Psychology.

Dr. RJ is the "go-to" professional for any and all topics pertaining to mental health. She has appeared as the expert psychologist on the Lifetime series Killer Kids and on several episodes of the docu-crime series For My Man on TV One, she is the host of Wellness Wednesday for KPRS Hot 103 Jamz in Kansas City, and she has au- thored several blogs and articles for a va- riety of publications. Dr. RJ has received numerous awards for her work in the field of psychology and prides herself on mak- ing the subject of psychology and men- tal health more relatable. Dr. RJ is also a certified Zumba instructor and is passionate about teaching the importance of the mind, body, spirit connection as it relates to total wellness.

s an African-American woman, Dr. RJ recognizes the unique impact of stress on her demographic. Author of the newly published book **Stress, Lies and Vacancy: The Self Care Guide to Refill Your Empty Vessel,** Dr. RJ's experiences and transparency provide an empowering self help guide for women of color to reduce common stressors in their lives that have long term effects on the body and brain. Through this latest endeavor Dr. RJ is on a mission to heal one woman at a time and debunk the myth of the Black superwoman. Although she absolutely loves her career, her ultimate joy comes from her faith in God, and her love for her husband and their two children. Dr. RJ's favorite quote is "Self-care isn't selfish. You can't serve from an empty vessel".

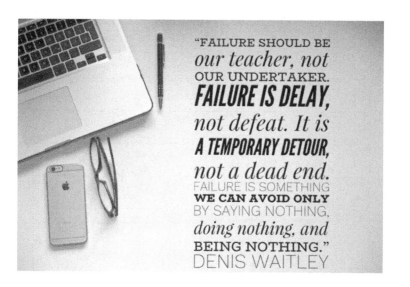

Journal

1. 10 cost-free things that make me feel
   happy:

2. My favorite quotes to live by:

3. Five things to do more of:

4. Five things to do less of:

5. What do I need to be content?

6. How would I like people to remember me after graduation?

7. 10 affirmations that remind me of who I am:

8. What would I say to my high school self?

9. If I had a superpower it would be...

10. What am I thankful for on a daily
basis?

Resources

Education and Consulting

Harbor Institute

A Premier Education Consulting Firm

theharborinstitute.com

info@theharborinstitute.com

Harbor Next

Professional Development

harbor-next.com

ni@harbor-next.com

First Generation Success

https://firstgen.naspa.org/

Find a Therapist Near You

- Psychologytoday.com
- Therapyforblackgirls.com
- Pridecounseling.com

Helplines

- National Suicide Prevention Helpline 1-800-273-8255

- National Domestic Violence Hotline (NCADV) | 1-800-799-7233

- National Alliance on Mental Illness (NAMI) 1-800-950-NAMI

- National Institute of Mental Health (NIMH) 1-866-615-6464

- National Sexual Assault Hotline (RAINN) 1-800-656-4673

- Substance Abuse and Mental Health Services: SAMHSA's National Helpline – 1-800-662-HELP (4357).

Mental Health Organizations

- American Psychological Association (APA) www.APA.org

- Anxiety and Depression Association of America (ADAA) https://adaa.org/find-help-for/women/anxiety

- National Institute of Mental Health

overwhelmed

(NIMH) https://www.nimh.nih.gov/health/topics/index.shtml

- Blackdoctor.org: https://blackdoctor.org/category/healthy-living/womens-health/

References

*For other cultural models of identity, see below:

Biracial Identity Model (Poston 1990)

Asian Identity Model (Sue and Sue)

White Identity Model (Helms)

Black Identity Model (Cross)

Ethnic Minority Identity Model (Berry)

Multiracial Identity Model (Root 1990, 2003)

Integrated Model (John and Joy Hoffman)

Cross, W. E. (1971). The Negro to Black conversion experience: Toward a psychology of Black liberation. Black World, 20, 13-27.

Helms, J. E. (1984). Towards a theoretical explanation of effects of race on counseling:

A Black and White model. Counseling Psychologist, 12, 153-165.

Kim J. (1981) The process of Asian American identity development from Sue, et al. (1998). Multicultural Counseling Competencies: Individual and Organizational Development. Sage Productions. Thousand Oaks, CA.

Ruiz (1990) from Sue, et al. (1998). Multicultural Counseling Competencies: Individual and Organizational Development. Sage Productions. Thousand Oaks, CA.

Sue, D. W. & Sue, D. (2016). Racial/Cultural Identity Development in people of color: Therapeutic implications, Chapter 11. In Sue, D.W. & Sue, D. (Eds.), Counseling the Culturally Diverse: Theory and Practice (7th ed.) Hoboken, NJ: Wiley.

Pop Quiz Answers

Page 8 - What is self-care?

(D) All of the above

Page 35 - Toxic or Typical?: **All of the situations listed in 1-10 are toxic**. These are all warning signs of depression, anxiety, or suicide, yet many students think that these symptoms are typical or common.

Page 72 - What is a neurotransmitter?

(A) Chemical Messenger

Image Attributions

Chalkboard: <ahref='https://www.freepik.com/photos/background'>Background photo created by rawpixel.com - www.freepik.com</a>

Endnotes

1. https://www.talentsmart.com/articles/ Multitasking-Damages-Your-Brain- and-Your-Creer,-New-Studies-Suggest- 2102500909-p-1.html

2. https://www.ncbi.nlm.nih.gov/pmc/ articles/PMC5536318/#:~:text=Up%20 to%2060%25%20of%20all,criteria%20 of%20an%20insomnia%20disorder.

3. https://www.psychiatry.org/pa- tients-families/adhd/what-is-adhd

4. https://www.psychiatry.org/pa- tients-families/adhd/what-is-adhd

5. https://www.mayoclinic.org/diseas- es-conditions/anxiety/symptoms-caus- es/syc-20350961

6. https://www.nimh.nih.gov/health/ publications/social-anxiety-disor- der-more-than-just-shyness/index.sht- ml

7. https://www.nimh.nih.gov/health/topics/depression/index.shtml

8. https://www.healthline.com/health/suicide-and-suicidal-behavior#suicidal-signs

9. https://www.samhsa.gov/find-help/atod

10. https://www.drugabuse.gov/publications/drugacts/hallucinogens

11. https://www.drugs.com/illicit/lsd.html

12. Ibid

13. https://www.cdc.gov/std/default.htm

14. https://www.cdc.gov/violenceprevention/intimatepartnerviolence/fastfact.html

15. https://www.cdc.gov/violenceprevention/intimatepartnerviolence/fastfact.html

16. https://www.womenshealth.gov/relationships-and-safety/

sexual-assault-and-rape/college-sexual-assault#:~:text=Sexual%20assault%20is%20common%20among,in%20college%20experiences%20sexual%20assault.&text=Studies%20show%20that%20students%20are,and%20second%20semesters%20in%20college.

17. https://www.youtube.com/watch?v=f-GoWLWS4-kU

18. Khan, Timothy, *Pathways: A Guided Workbook for Youth Beginning Treatment*, Fourth Edition

19. https://www.verywellmind.com/the-id-ego-and-superego-2795951

20. Ibid.

21. https://www.ncbi.nlm.nih.gov/books/NBK556096/

22. https://www.webmd.com/children/piaget-stages-of-development#1

23. https://www.racialequitytools.org/resourcefiles/

Compilation_of_Racial_Identity_
Models_7_15_11.pdf

24. https://www.npr.
org/2020/06/08/872371063/microag-
gressions-are-a-big-deal-how-to-talk-
them-out-and-when-to-walk-away

25. https://tlexinstitute.com/how-to-ef-
fortlessly-have-more-posi-
tive-thoughts/#:~:text=Tendencies%20
of%20the%20mind&text=It%20was%20
found%20that%20the,thoughts%20
as%20the%20day%20before.

For more information visit:

askdrrj.com

selfcareforthecollegestudent.com

Made in the USA
Monee, IL
20 September 2021